STOCK MARKETS OF THE ARAB WORLD

Ayman Shafiq Fayyad Abdul-Hadi, Department of Economics, University of Exeter.

Foreign interest in the oil producing Arab countries has grown recently due to the accumulation of international reserves. Oil producers are looking for an alternative to their near term investments in United States Securities through a diversification of their economies. This book argues that these countries could profitably invest these reserves through an integration of their securities markets. Attempts at such integration have been made by Arab countries but many obstacles stood in the way and few benefits were derived from the various agreements. Nevertheless, it is argued, prospects for increased linkages among the Arab domestic markets do exist.

This book provides a sound description and analysis of the stock markets in the Arab World and an evaluation of previous attempts at the integration of capital markets. It also explores the prospects for capital market integration among Arab countries based on the integration of their securities markets.

STOCK MARKETS OF THE ARAB WORLD:

Trends, Problems and Prospects for Integration

AYMAN SHAFIQ FAYYAD ABDUL-HADI

ROUTLEDGE
London and New York

First published in 1988 by
Routledge
11 New Fetter Lane, London EC4P 4EE

Published in the USA by
Routledge
in association with Routledge, Chapman & Hall, Inc.
29 West 35th Street, New York NY 10001

© 1988 A.S. Abdul Hadi

Printed in Great Britain by Billing & Sons Ltd, Worcester

British Library Cataloguing in Publication Data

Abdul-Hadi, Ayman Shafiq
    Stock markets of the Arab world: trends,
    problems and prospects for integration.
    1. Stock-exchange — Arab countries
    I. Title
    332.64′2174927   HG5712
    ISBN 0-415-00335-0

Library of Congress Cataloging-in-Publication Data

    ISBN 0-415-00335-0

CONTENTS

Contents

TABLES

FIGURES

I dedicate this work to my family;

To my father whose constant encouragement kept me going.
My mother, who gave so much of her life, and to my aunt
who was a second mother to me.

FOREWORD

Rodney Wilson

In the development literature there is a new stress on the need to harness private venture capital, and international bodies such as the World Bank advocate an increased role for private investors in the finance of industrialisation. Arab governments are rediscovering the merits of equity finance, and even in countries where the state provided most investment funds in the past, the contribution of free enterprise is now being welcomed.

Ayman Abdul-Hadi's study is timely in view of these developments, as it is the only comprehensive review of stock markets throughout the Arab world. There is much to be learnt from the contrasting experiences of the stock markets in Kuwait, Manama, Jeddah, Amman, Beirut, Cairo, Casablanca and Tunis. The author explains how each of these markets developed and evolved, and many parallels are evident in their roles and operations, despite the differing economic environments and variations in historical context.

The Egyptian market is, of course, the oldest, dating from the nineteenth century, and it is interesting to ask why it did not play a greater role in the country's development, as it pre-dates many European markets which ultimately became much more significant. The Kuwaiti stock market attracted much media attention in the aftermath of the Souk Al-Manakh crisis, but little has been written about activity in Bahrain and Saudi Arabia, although their domestic markets were an alternative to dealing in Gulf offshore companies. The Amman market is one of the most interesting, as it has been less volatile than Kuwait's and private quoted companies play a major role in Jordan's economy. As there is little written in English on the Beirut, Casablanca and Tunis markets, Ayman Abdul-Hadi's account is particularly informative for the Western reader.

The degree of economic integration in the Arab world is limited, but links are strongest at the factor market rather than the traded goods level, with much mobility of both labour and capital between Arab countries. Ayman Abdul-Hadi proposes strengthening these capital linkages, so that Arab investors will be less inclined to place funds in London or Wall Street. A balanced and diversified asset portfolio can be established for both individual and institutional investors by holding equity investments in different Arab markets. The Arab World is so diverse that adverse price trends in one market can be offset by bullish movements in another. Yet many wealthy investors in the Gulf have not seriously considered the possibility and opportunities in the Arab world, where they can exploit their superior insider knowledge to identify the most promising investments. It is after all within the Arab world that they have a comparative advantage over Western investors, not in the city of London or New York.

This book represents a sound piece of academic research, and it is evident that Ayman Abdul-Hadi is well versed in the theory of finance, and has an excellent understanding of how equity markets function in practice. It is hoped that more young Arab scholars will undertake work in this field in the years ahead. Ultimately, the Arab countries must have both width and depth in their financial markets if they are to develop economically viable enterprises that can compete successfully in world markets.

Rodney Wilson: Pro-Director, Centre for Middle Eastern and Islamic Studies and Senior Lecturer in the Economics of the Middle East, University of Durham

ACKNOWLEDGEMENTS

Many thanks go to Dr Alexandra Hardie, whose ideas and opinions helped in shaping this work and to whom I owe an enormous debt.

Many thanks also to the staff of the University of Exeter Library, the Amman Financial Market and the Kuwaiti Stock Exchange for their assistance in providing material for this work.

INTRODUCTION

In recent years, foreign interest in the oil-producing Arab countries has grown rapidly. This has, in part, been contributed to by the accumulation of international reserves by these countries. Thus, the oil producers would like, through a diversification of their economies, to encourage other sectors of income that will promote economic growth in the future.

While those countries are planning near-term investments in United States securities, securities of US companies, US treasury bonds and other debt issues, the oil-producing countries realise that such an investment offers only a short-term outlet for their surplus funds. Thus, their search to find an alternative.

Although the West is concerned with the oil money and would like to see more of the oil revenues channelled into investment in their own countries, investment in the economies of the West does not solve the long-term problem of minimising the dependence on oil through diversification. Recently, the focus has been on Arab capital market integration, encouraged by the structural differences in the Arab region that were magnified by the oil financial surplus. The factor-mix in the various Arab countries divides them into two groups: the capital-abundant but labour-scarce oil exporting countries, and the deficit Arab countries which carry the opposite characteristics. Whereas the former are accumulating liquid assets far in excess of their present ability to absorb capital, the latter are suffering from a lack of capital while displaying a greater capital absorptive capacity. The challenge, therefore, lies in harmonising the long-term investment interests of the surplus countries with the development needs and economic potentials of the capital-needy countries. To reach this goal, financial assistance, though necessary, is only a temporary move. There is a great need to encourage the capacity of the deficit countries to attract investors on a commercial basis. One way in which those objectives could be met is through integrating these countries' securities markets.

The purpose of this study is to explore the prospects for capital market integration among the Arab countries of the Middle East, based on integration of their securities markets. The first step towards the goal of financial integration is to determine the size of the markets of the region involved in order to see whether the enlargement of these markets is financially feasible. Specifically, one would like to know if the integration of these markets is justifiable.

In short, this study attempts to show that one way of achieving steady regional economic growth in the long-run is through financial integration among the Arab countries of the Middle East. The first step towards this goal is the establishment of a scheme of partial integration; securities market integration. It is hoped that once the economic benefits of such integration are shown, then it would help to overcome the political obstacles which stand in the way of economic integration.

As the conditions for complete economic integration among the Arab countries do not exist at the present time, this study will concentrate on a limited, more realistic, integration scheme which, once established, will pave the way for bigger schemes.

Studies of the Middle East cannot ignore the volatile situation in the area, and the future unpredictability of this region. The problems include the Arab-Israeli conflict, the Lebanese civil war, the Iraq-Iran war and others. As the present study is concerned with long-term prospects for economic development, people wonder whether it is realistic to think in terms of long-term planning in such a turbulent region. However, the fact remains that the Arab oil-producing countries with their oil revenues are looking for new venues in which they can profitably invest these reserves.

Before embarking on the discussion, it will be helpful to define exactly what is meant by the terms that will recur constantly.

Introduction

1. Financial market

A financial market consists of a number of subsectors - money markets and capital markets.

(a) Money market is a market for short-term credit, such as short-term government securities, commercial paper, bankers' acceptances, inter-bank loans, negotiable certificates.
(b) Capital market is a market for long-term credit which takes the form of common stock, bonds and mortgage instruments.

2. Securities markets

As part of capital market is defined as business done in securities (primarily shares and bonds), which are negotiable and thus enable an investment to be converted into cash before its term, which is generally medium or long. There are two distinct markets for shares and for bonds within any securities markets, with substantially different functions. The share market enables investors taking an interest in the capital of a company to raise venture capital, while the bond markets enable capital to be raised or invested in the form of borrowing or lending. Each of these markets is organised into two sections:

(a) The primary market represented by the aggregate of new securities issues over a given time period. It allows capital to be mobilised and issuers to place their stock with investors.
(b) The secondary market in which securities already in issue are traded. This market provides a vehicle for realising financial wealth invested in securities and the degree to which it works directly affects the primary market, as it determines to what extent securities are liquid.

3. Stock exchange

These are institutions whose main objective is to provide an efficient secondary market. They offer the facilities required for the purchase and sale of newly issued securities, bringing together buyers and sellers, who determine the prices freely and competitively.

4. Parallel market

Quoted securities traded outside the stock exchange.

This study is organised into five chapters. In the introduction we have briefly discussed the background of the study with emphasis on economic integration in the form of partial integration (capital market) as being the most practical way to start the process that might lead later to complete integration.

In the first chapter, we will discuss the existing literature on economic integration, monetary integration and capital market integration.

In the second, third and fourth chapters we will concentrate on the structures of the securities markets of the countries in our study.

Chapter 5 investigates the prospects and problems for integration. The main task is to examine the need for financial integration among the Arab countries and to determine the appropriate path to pursue. Previous attempts at integration are evaluated and the measures taken to integrate Arab capital markets are outlined. It has been found that no benefits have been derived from the various agreements that have been signed. The flow of capital from the existing Arab funds to industrial and Arab countries is analysed to determine whether links among the capital markets of the Arab countries do exist. Also, the obstacles to the strengthening of inter-market relationships will be mentioned.

The conclusion will give a summary and overview of the study as a whole, in addition to future recommendations on what course to follow for the integration of these markets.

Chapter One

THEORIES OF INTEGRATION

I   ECONOMIC INTEGRATION

The literal meaning of the term 'integration' denotes the 'bringing together of parts into a whole'. However, in reviewing the literature on economic integration, we find that the concept has been interpreted broadly. A common definition of economic integration agreed upon by economists has been absent, which in turn gives the term an ambiguous meaning.

One economist who defines integration in a broad and vague manner is Gunnar Myrdal. His definition centres around the ideal of equality of opportunity. According to Myrdal, integration is a social and economic process which destroys barriers between the participants. In national integration 'the economy is not integrated unless all avenues are open to everybody and the remunerations paid for productive services are equal'. (1) While in international economic integration Myrdal defines the concept as 'the realisation of the same ideal of equality of opportunity in the relations between peoples of different nations'. (2)

This definition has its attraction if economic integration is thought of in terms of welfare effects with its ideal of equal opportunity. However, putting the concept of economic integration within this framework gives it a vague meaning, since its job of equalising factor prices in different parts of the market has so far not worked in any market. So, even if we do agree that social integration is necessary for total integration, what is more important for economic integration is the removal of trade restrictions in customs unions, free trade areas and common markets.

1

Bela Balassa, with more precision, attempts to define economic integration both as a process and as a state of affairs. As a process, economic integration 'encompasses measures designed to abolish discrimination between economic units belonging to different national states'. As a state of affairs, 'it can be represented by the absence of various forms of discrimination between national economies'. (3)

Balassa also proposes a distinction between trade integration, factor integration, policy integration and total integration, which economists attacked for different reasons. Machlup criticised this concept on the grounds that Balassa restricted the process or state of affairs to different nations joining in a regional group or bloc. Machlup proposes, in addition to the abolishment of discriminatory barriers among a group of countries, an inter-weaving and inter-dependence of all or part of their economic activities in both the regional economy and that of its constituent units. (4) Machlup's definition implies increasing the inter-connections of the structures of consumption and of production, and the utilisation of all productive resources which are available in the region. These would not occur without a social and economic transformation and co-ordination of policies. Thus, the goal of integration is not to eliminate barriers but also to create incentives for development. Another critic is Imre Vajdo, who criticised Balassa because his definition 'restricts integration entirely to the market level'. (5)

This confusion of concepts regarding the term economic integration and its stages of development might lead to a wrong interpretation of the results of the development of this integration process. For instance, since socialist countries are different in their characteristics, stages of development and mechanisms for the market system, they do not have to make use of methods such as free trade zones or customs unions, but rather 'through the co-ordination of national economic plans and ... solely on administrative non-market means'. (6) Another criticism of Balassa's definition is seen in its applicability to developing economies. In this respect, the concept of integration is not just the lifting of trade restrictions but also the inspiration of economic development, where the process of development is defined as the 'diversification induced in the production structure and in industrialization, a union might very well need more protection than that available to the participants individually prior to the establishment of the union'. (7) So policy co-ordination is a necessary instrument in the earlier stages of the integration processes. (8)

The concept of economic integration took a comprehensive form when defined by Pinder as 'both the removal of discrimination as between the economic agents of the member countries, and the formation and application of co-ordinated and common policies on a sufficient scale to ensure that major economic and welfare objectives are fulfilled'. (9) However, Pinder's definition is criticised by Imre Vajdo because it does not give a sharp enough definition of the limits of integration. Thus, Vajdo makes a distinction between what he calls 'market integration' and 'production and development integration'. He defines the former as 'the guarantee of unhindered sale of each other's products within the framework of the social system of participating countries', (10) while the latter involves 'raising to an international level and programming the production of those branches of industry which cannot be developed to an optimum size within national boundaries without upsetting the internal equilibrium of the national economy'. (11) To Vajdo, the former is supplemented by the latter and is applied to socialist developed markets and to developing countries.

Economic integration which, as we have seen, has been defined differently, falls into five stages: free trade area, customs union, common market, economic union and complete economic integration.

(1) In the free trade area participant countries abolish tariffs and quantitative restrictions on trade between themselves, while each country retains its own tariff against non-members. The free trade area has a disadvantage in that it is possible for commodities to move from outside the region into the area through the country that has the lowest tariff, thus reducing the protectionism effects of the higher tariffs of the other member countries. In this case, regulations are needed concerning the origin of goods and close administration for implementation.

(2) In a customs union, the above problem is solved through the adoption of a common external tariff on non-members, in addition to free trade between members. But, as a uniform external tariff will cause a shift in the cost of production and pattern of trade within the region, it becomes necessary for the community to compensate the

injured country.

(3) The next stage of integration is that of a common market. This type embodies the abolishment of impediments and restrictions on factor movements within the area. Also, it involves not only the promotion of trade between member countries, but the encouragement of specialisation and co-operation in productive sectors.

(4) A developed stage of economic integration is the economic union. This stage goes beyond the scope of the common market through the partial adoption of unified and multilateral economic policies.

(5) The highest stage of economic integration is that of total economic integration. It involves, in addition to trade and factoral movements and co-ordination, unified monetary, fiscal, social and counter-cyclical policies, which 'require the setting up of a supranational authority whose decisions are binding for the member states'. (12) Economic integration need not embrace all sectors of the economy. Partial integration, limited to one sector, is a more promising form of integration among developing countries. Most developing countries have not gone into their integrative efforts beyond the formation of customs unions. They tend to be sensitive to factor mobility (capital). Of the several sectors of economic integration, monetary integration is our next topic of discussion. Our interest lies in this form of partial integration since it has a large bearing on our main interest: capital market integration.

II MONETARY INTEGRATION

We now shift to a survey of the conceptual and theoretical aspects of monetary integration. The term 'monetary integration' which, according to Machlup, 'is an integral part of complete economic integration' (13), is defined in its simplest form as 'an arrangement between a number of countries to maintain an agreed exchange rate between their currencies' (14) or, in other words, the establishment of a regional payments system that allows payments and foreign exchange transactions without restrictions or control. The European monetary system would satisfy this definition 'as capital for direct investment, for acquiring an interest in a business or in property, as well as personal savings, can today move within the EEC from one country to another without any major restrictions from exchange regulations'. (15) The same could be said of investment in stocks and shares where previously controlled operations were freed. To Machlup, this establishment of arrangements that facilitate foreign payments is the essence of monetary integration, the way being the replacement of separate national currencies by a common currency to be used throughout the area. Although other writers agree with Machlup's definition of monetary integration in terms of the establishment of a common currency, the 1970 Werner report (16) challenges this practice by treating full and irrevocable fixing of exchange rates as equivalent to the adoption of a common currency. Here, it is argued that provided exchange rates really are irrevocably fixed, the private sector would be guilty of money illusion if it treated currencies differently just because they had different names and denominations.

However, Corden disagrees with this argument and argues that if separate currencies continue to exist, then the credibility of irrevocably fixed exchange rates is questionable, as it is easy to break such a promise. In this respect, the private sector could not be persuaded to believe that exchange rates were irrevocably fixed by any 'pseudo exchange-rate union', which would mean that capital movement would still be impeded by risk aversion. This reasoning is generally accepted and, as such, monetary integration will be interpreted as the adoption of a single currency. To elaborate more on the term, Corden regards monetary integration as consisting of two essential components. The first component is the exchange-rate union, that is 'an area within which exchange rates bear a permanently fixed relationship to each other even though the rates may - in unison - vary relative to non-union currencies', while the second component is convertibility which is 'the permanent absence of all exchange controls, whether for current or capital transactions, within the area', (17) including interest and dividend payments. Convertibility for capital transactions is an important aspect of capital market integration, that is 'the establishment of a unified capital market with no geographic restrictions of any kind on capital movements within the area'. (18) Therefore, monetary integration is regarded as consisting of two related components, an exchange-rate union accompanied by a capital-market integration, the latter being of concern to us.

Bela Balassa agrees with Machlup on the idea of full

monetary integration but whereas Machlup means by it the existence of a common currency, Balassa introduces three systems to be adopted until the conditions for the permanent fixing of exchange rates are fulfilled. These are adjustable pegs, full flexible exchange rates and the crawling peg. (19) The latter is defined as

a term used in connection with foreign exchange when the monetary authorities of a country decide to maintain or peg the rate of exchange of their currency at a fixed rate. The term is also sometimes used of the control of prices. (20)

These alternatives given by Balassa take the place of the undesirability of adopting fixed exchange rates. Balassa argues that uncertainties in transactions of exchange in nominal and real exchange rates and inefficiencies in resource allocation can be reduced if fluctuations in real exchange rates are avoided. After adopting the system of crawling pegs to accomplish the previous results, the creation of a common currency would follow, 'around which the currencies of individual member countries could fluctuate'. (21)

Other discussions of monetary integration have been concerned with changes less radical than the establishment of a single currency. They refer to the form of joint monetary action by countries having different currencies as 'partial monetary integration', of which seven forms have appeared in the literature.

Payment union is an arrangement between countries with inconvertible currencies to set up a multilateral clearing arrangement to handle payments for their reciprocal trade to eliminate any discrimination in trade between countries of the payment union.

Reserve pooling is where a part of the members' reserves is deposited with an agent, and where members acquire liquid claims on the agent, who in turn holds liquid claims on third parties. The agents can extend credit within certain limits and without putting the liquidity of their members' deposits in jeopardy.

Exchange-rate co-ordination constitutes an agreement between members to conduct policies to limit the extent of diverging the exchange rates between currencies of the participant countries. As such, what is needed is the establishment of 'central rates' between members' currencies and obligation to restrict deviations from those central rates by means of interventionist policies.

Monetary co-ordination: among the various types of policy co-ordination, the most important one is an agreement as to the monetary policies that member countries will pursue. These vary between monetary policies in terms of the adoption of common interest rate targets or, in countries with floating exchange rates, in focusing on a target for some concepts of the money supply, or a target for domestic credit expansion. In countries with pegged exchange rates, monetary policy has come to mean domestic credit expansion.

Parallel currency is a currency set up in the region to supplement and not to substitute for existing currencies.

Capital market integration refers to steps taken to increase capital mobility, one of which is the abolition of exchange controls on capital flows within the area and the harmonisation of administrative requirements in financial matters.

Common policies toward external capital flows include the possibilities of standardising policy regarding capital flows to and from the world, liberalising capital movements within the integrated area and taking joint action to channel financial surpluses into investment outside the area.

III CAPITAL MARKET INTEGRATION

According to Machlup, the capital market is where medium and long-term securities are traded. 'The capital markets are chiefly stock exchanges and bond markets but also various supplementary markets in which a variety of financial assets of deferred maturity were exchanged against money.' (22) These money markets deal in money market instruments, including promissory notes, bills, certificates of deposits, acceptances, loans on maturities ranging from overnight money to six-month credits, and so on.

Capital market integration is defined in its broadest

sense as integration of the complex of machinery through which funds are collected and channelled towards the financing of productive investment and of economic and social infrastructures. Capital market integration does not only mean full capital mobility among the parts of the union. It also 'implies the replacement of separate regulatory frameworks by one central machinery for the regulation of credit interest rates, financial institutions and securities business'. (23) In short, capital market integration refers to the steps taken to increase capital mobility of which the abolition of exchange controls on capital flows within the area is the most important. (24) The second important aspect of it is the harmonisation of administration requirements in financial matters to facilitate the operation of financial intermediaries who operate across national frontiers, and the sale of financial obligations to savers resident not in the country of issue. In short, capital market integration is a 'mechanism to bring borrowers and lenders together which is more effective than the present system of separate and relatively thin domestic security markets subject to individual and distinct control by the national governments'. (25)

Capital market integration falls into three categories; regional capital-market integration, worldwide capital-market integration and national market integration, i.e. segmented. Regional integration is where integration occurs between several national capital markets within a regional framework, while worldwide integration is where this happens on a worldwide basis.

There are several factors that work against worldwide capital-market integration. One is the preference given to investment at home over investment abroad. A large number of financial centres prefer to invest abroad, either to evade taxation or because of exchange considerations. In the face of such movements, governments of capital-losing countries put barriers against the outflow of domestic financial resources which tend to limit the freedom of capital movements.

Another factor is the protection of the balance of payments which the liberalisation of capital movements might harm. Governments have recently become aware that large capital outflows put huge pressure on their external balance. That is why governments introduced restrictive measures on investments abroad.

A third factor is that it would endanger the autonomy

of national monetary and financial policies. Here, the authorities have to ensure that freedom of capital movements will not endanger their economic policy and ability to guide the flow of savings into preferred channels of investment. But it is not just government action that prevents such integration, ignorance of overseas opportunities might also be a factor. Thus, these three factors prevent the integration of capital markets on a worldwide basis.

Within the first category - regional integration of national capital markets - consideration is given to tax, currency and cyclical policy in addition to the three factors mentioned above. In capital-market integration, holders of securities issues in the various countries are treated equally through 'the rules applicable to the taxation of income on domestic and foreign securities, the system of withholding taxes, and the way in which interest or dividends paid are reported to the tax administration'. (26) Another difficulty concerns the addition of exchange controls, where there is exchange risk on long-term capital transactions for which no forward cover can be obtained. The last difficulty lies in the uneasy task of harmonising the levels of economic activities between various economies.

Further disadvantages concerning this type of capital market integration are:

(1) the loss of monetary autonomy, for 'monetary authorities have to make sure that an excessive freedom of capital movements will not deprive them of a crucial weapon of their economic policy'. (27) In such a system of freedom of capital movements, a rise in interest rates and tightening of money market conditions would attract an inflow of foreign capital, offsetting any monetary contraction;

(2) in the absence of exchange restrictions, the movement of capital will be governed by differences in earning possibilities and by the estimated degree of risk and uncertainty, and

(3) it has also been argued that the benefits of allowing creditors to distribute their assets widely could be gained at the cost of a tendency to draw investment away from the weaker members of the group, and give it 'to the most developed regions in order to take advantage of their infrastructure and more highly qualified work force', (28) thus tightening the external

constraint on economic policy in those countries and reducing their potential growth.

Nevertheless, a regional capital-market integration has several advantages of which greater size is the most important as it increases efficiency and adaptability and reduces costs. In this case, private persons and institutions can expand their investment opportunities as 'a joint capital market affords a far greater potential than is now available in the various separate national markets'. (29) Such an integrated capital market would reduce inequalities in the conditions of competition by 'giving companies access to sources of financing on equal terms throughout the region', (30) and 'requires that firms in each member country have access on equal terms to the savings of all'. (31)

Moreover, integration would lead banks and other institutions in isolated capital markets to dilute their monopolistic powers. It would also give broader and deeper securities markets, thus enhancing the liquidity of seasonal securities and reducing the cost of borrowing.

Integration would also improve the allocational efficiency of the financial process. This means that investors would be faced with a broader spectrum of risk-return opportunities, while borrowers would face an end to relative scarcity of resources. There is also a resource-allocation benefit of allowing investment to occur where rates of return are highest rather than where savings are being affected.

Firms that could be financially efficient would increase in size; there would arise the need for a large-scale inflow of external resources due to the competitive situation, advancing technology, and increasing factor costs. In this case, an integrated capital market is needed for providing finance for large firms to keep up their growth and competitiveness.

The integration of capital markets benefits investors because any expansion in their opportunity improves their welfare. The merging of capital markets leads to changes in the risk-return price relationship, which in return brings positive improvement to an individual's wealth. '... international capital-market integration is pareto-optimal i.e. the welfare of individuals in the economies considered never declines, and will generally improve'. (32)

Within a capital-market integration, when capital is highly mobile, monetary policy can be assigned to regulate the balance of payments, freeing other policy instruments for the pursuit of domestic objectives. It will also reduce market imperfections and international differences in taxation.

Capital-market integration is too broad a concept and there are many obstacles to its achievement. To create links between national markets one must start with specific markets, of which integration of the securities markets is, for many reasons, the best choice.

Securities markets are markets that would become more efficient through integration, leading to bigger size and economies of scale. For example, one of the main characteristics of the Arab security markets is their narrowness. There are several reasons, historical, sociological and technical; savers are reluctant to invest in securities, especially in shares; some family group companies put a limited proportion of the equity capital on the market; finance companies sometimes keep stocks in their portfolios and thus have a low turnover; the large volume of business traded outside the market. 'The widening of the market to be obtained by the removal of existing barriers and by giving greater freedom of action to institutional investors, would ensure greater stability both of issue conditions and subsequent price movements.' (33)

The integration of the Arab securities markets means essentially 'standardisation of practices with and between, and removal of controls over, those markets', (34) which obviously means a great number of reforms to eliminate differences in tax systems, trading costs, various types of markets, orders and operations, guarantees, nature of securities listed and traded, and the quality and channels of financial information.

Conditions for the creation of a large regional stock market

The first steps towards integration would include:

1. Legal aspects of the process of integration: in the legal field, one aspect is negotiation for the harmonisation of the law as to prospectuses and the directives aimed at removing restrictions on the capital market. Another is to remove all discriminating measures which create obstacles to the right of establishment for companies and legal bodies. Companies should be given the right to form subsidiaries in the

11

different countries of the integrated area without being subjected to discriminatory impediments. Other aspects include the harmonisation of the publications which companies have to issue; harmonisation of the conditions of subscription of capital as well as of dividends, the purchase by a company of its own shares, reductions of capital, and so on. The creation of a legal entity, the Arab grouping of economic interests, whose purpose is to carry out joint ventures between small and medium-sized companies from different member countries. Although the legal aspect is difficult, it is the basis of everything in the process of integration.

2. Fiscal aspects of a security market: as the lack of fluidity of capital is due to tax considerations, the objective of an integrated security market is to create a fiscal system. 'Tax neutrality means that taxes affect neither the choice of the place of investment on transaction nor the saver's choice between making the investment direct or using the services of a financial intermediary.' (35) The Segre report also called for the improvement of tax systems: abolition of double taxation; elimination of tax disadvantages attached to investment effected in other member countries though the intermediary of financial institutions; amendment of the 'tax credit' systems to remove the fiscal advantages reserved for investment in particular countries; harmonisation of treatment of dividends and interest paid to non-residents. This harmonisation either takes the form of total abolition of withholding on bond interest on the application of a uniform rate of tax throughout the community, or discrimination against non-resident investors in subjecting them to corporate taxation, encouraging savers to invest in their own countries and not abroad.

3. Operations and regulations of stock markets: in addition to other improvements, the development of an integrated securities market calls for 'action to adopt security dealing techniques on official and unofficial markets and to create the conditions for securities to circulate as freely throughout the community as within a domestic market'. (36) One of these conditions is to lengthen official stock exchange lists in member countries, by introducing foreign securities on each stock exchange. Whereas it could be argued that savers must be protected in case of introduction of foreign securities, the fact is that this 'often masks a desire to reserve the market's resources for domestic

enterprises'. (37) Moreover, this view fails to recognise other aspects such as: admission to stock exchange quotation does not in fact mean placement of a new issue - it could denote the recognition of an existing situation, that is, residents already hold a large number of foreign securities; admission of a large number of securities from other member countries would lower the cost of transactions in these securities, which is higher than for similar dealings in domestic securities. This is because a transaction on a foreign stock exchange incurs not only ordinary costs, but expenses of correspondents abroad, on exchange commission and double taxation.

Another condition is to develop trading in foreign securities outside the official markets by allowing any security officially listed and traded in any member country to be automatically eligible for unofficial trading in other member countries without any formalities.

A further condition is to harmonise market practices and price-quotation techniques. As different systems of price quotation are employed in member countries, a first step towards harmonisation would be the co-ordination of trading hours on the various markets, thus facilitating arbitrage operations. Some countries quote their shares in terms of percentage of nominal value, others in terms of money units. Investors, even those 'familiar with the machinery in their own domestic market often find it difficult to read and interpret foreign quotations'. (38) In this case, harmonisation would be very important.

Still another condition is to unify the rules governing intermediary activities on stock exchanges. In order to have important public benefits such as efficient market pricing and mobilisation of savings for capital formation, a system of stock exchange monopoly for security trading is desirable. Investors should have access to publication of quotes and prices information on share movements and on general market activity, as well as financial information on listed securities and companies. As for banks and credit institutions, it would be beneficial for them to act as intermediaries in stock exchange business. Thus, it would be necessary to harmonise the rules of bank operations on equity markets, as their activities would contribute to the integration process, 'since the banks could acquire the necessary knowledge of business and stock exchange machinery in the partner countries more easily than other investors'. (39) In contrast to the short-term business of banks in the UK and USA, where banks are not important as intermediaries on the stock markets, the financial institutions being insurance and pension funds and investment and unit trust, in the Arab region banks play an important role on the stock exchange because of the liquidity of oil money surplus.

Another condition is to design a unified system of supervision and regulation. For the market to reach a high standard of efficiency, investors should have confidence in the market. Investors are unlikely to have confidence in the market if intermediaries are not of good quality, if unsatisfactory procedures operate and if information is inadequate. To ensure confidence in the market, intermediaries and other stock exchange members should be supervised. Supervision should ensure that members have fairly basic knowledge of business, control the accounts of member firms to ensure that they pay back what money they owe, and should probably also 'extend regulation of certain procedures, for example, the manner in which clients' securities are held and the circumstances in which securities can be pledged as collateral'. (40)

The market must be wide enough to accommodate and offer a wide variety of securities. It also must be deep, in that it must have the capacity to supply and absorb substantial qualities of the different traded securities. Here, the supervisory body must ensure that listing applications are not made by issuers whose securities are controlled by one group. It must also check that the market is capable of absorbing large quantities of securities. The depth of the market is influenced by the type of information given to the public, which, when sufficient, should encourage interest in investment. Although this need not be inside the area of supervision, nevertheless it 'may be advantageous for supervisory authority to maintain a close liaison with the public relations organizations of the stock exchange'. (41) There must also be an adequate code of conduct in market dealings to ensure that every investor receives equitable treatment.

A further condition is to develop international brokerage firms which are important in an integrated securities market, as these are able to trade in the various countries without any constraints. They have 'to organise themselves to compete effectively in offering a number of essential services in the area of execution capability, securities research, and financial-advisory services to the investment public and to corporations that need to raise capital'. (42) These firms should have the expertise in selling securities business and in handling currency transactions.

Still another condition is to extend the jobbing system to enable the market to operate properly. While the value of shares represents a provision of income or capital growth to the investor, the value of a security to the jobber is the price at which he expects to sell in a short time. Because the jobber's role is different, this system is important to the market as it gives a high degree of liquidity, since the jobber ensures market availability to the public. The jobbing system is essential for regulating the market and preventing sharp disturbances. By anticipating the market trends, the jobber is able to prevent the price getting out of control and confine market fluctuations.

Types of securities in a unified market

Different markets have two forms of securities: the bearer form and the registered form. On some markets, the holders of securities may withhold their identity from the public by not registering on the stock exchange. In an integrated market there should be an agreement on a common practice in the transfer of stocks and shares between countries with different methods of issue. There should also be harmonisation of the types of securities offered so as to increase market activity. This is necessary because firms which are controlled by one family group do not always quote their securities on the stock exchange so as to keep control of the companies.

To develop a security clearing system

The clearing of transaction in securities should be put in the hands of specialist organisations which are linked together through direct relations, as witnessed from the American experience where 'the employment of a modern central depository system would increase the industry's capacity to handle a large volume of business and, at the same time, reduce bankers operating costs'. (43)

Information for the public

Developing an integrated securities market should be accompanied by improved and extended information for the public. As companies do not provide sufficient information, investors are discouraged from entering the equity market and this helps to keep the stock market narrow. Furthermore, investors tend to attach more importance to political events and tax considerations, rather than to developments within the company.

NOTES

1. Myrdal, G. (1956) <u>An international economy</u>, New York: Harper and Row, p. 11.
2. Ibid. p. 13.
3. Balassa, B. (1962) <u>The theory of economic integration</u>, London: George Allen and Unwin, p. 1.
4. Machlup, F. (1977) <u>A history of thought on economic integration</u>, New York: Macmillan Press, p. 65.
5. Vajdo, I. (ed.), (1971) 'Integration, economic union and national state' in <u>Foreign trade in a planned economy</u>, Cambridge: Cambridge University Press, p. 33.
6. Balassa, B. (1961) 'Towards a theory of economic integration', <u>Kyklos</u>, vol. 14, no. 3.
7. Wionczek, M. (1966) 'Introduction: requisites for viable integration' in Wionczek, M., <u>Latin American economic integration</u> (ed.), New York: Praeger Publishers, p. 8.
8. Kitamura, H. (1966) 'Economic theory and economic integration of under-developed regions' in Wionczek, M., <u>Latin American economic integration</u> (ed.) New York: Praeger Publishers, p. 45.
9. Pinder, J. (1968) 'Positive integration and negative integration: some problems of economic union in the EEC', <u>The World Today</u>, vol. 24, no. 3, March.
10. Vajdo, I. (1971) (ed.) 'Integration, economic union and national state' in <u>Foreign trade in a planned economy</u>, Cambridge: Cambridge University Press, p. 34.
11. Ibid. p. 35.
12. Balassa, B. (1962) <u>The theory of economic integration</u>, London: George Allen and Unwin, p. 2.
13. Machlup, F. (1977) <u>A history of thought on economic integration</u>, New York: Macmillan Press, p. 20.

14.   Hanson, J. (1977) A dictionary of economics and commerce, London: Macdonald Evans, p. 318.

15.   Segre, C. (1963) 'Financial markets in the EEC: prospects for integration', Moorgate and Wall Street, August.

16.   Werner, (1970) Rapport au conseil et à la Commission sur la réalisation par étapes de l'union économique et monetaire de la Communauté, 8 October, Supplement au Bulletin des Communautés Européennes, 11.

17.   Corden, W. (1972) Monetary integration: essays in international finance, no. 93, New Jersey: Princeton University, p. 2.

18.   Ibid. p. 2.

19.   Balassa, B. (1975) 'Monetary integration in the European capital market' in Balassa, B., European economic integration (ed.), New York, American Elsevier Publishing Company Inc., p. 205.

20.   Hanson, J. (1977) A dictionary of economics and commerce, London: Macdonald and Evans, p. 361.

21.   Balassa, B. (1975) 'Monetary integration in the European capital market' in Balassa, B., European economic integration (ed.), New York: American Elsevier Publishing Company Inc., p. 220.

22.   Machlup, F. (1977) A history of thought on economic integration, New York: Macmillan Press, p. 71.

23.   Betrand, R. (1976) 'Opening statement for group discussion' in Machlup, F., Economic integration worldwide, regional, sectoral (ed.), New York: Macmillan Press, p. 212.

24.   Williamson, J. (1980) 'On the concepts, objectives and modalities of monetary integration' in Haseeb, K. and Makdisi, S., Arab monetary integration (ed.), London: Croom Helm, p. 14.

25.   Williams, D. (1965) 'The development of capital markets in Europe', International Monetary Fund Staff Paper, xii, March.

26.   Larre, R. (1969) 'Facts of life about the integration of national capital markets', Journal of Money, Credit and Banking, vol. 1, no. 3, August.

27.   Ibid.

28.   Segre, C. (1963) 'Financial markets in the EEC: prospects for integration', Moorgate and Wall Street, August.

29.   Richebecher, K. (1969) 'The problems and prospects of integration in European capital markets', Journal of Money, Credit and Banking, vol. 1, no. 3, August.

30. Schmitt, H. (1969) 'Capital markets and the unification of Europe', World Politics, vol. 20, no. 2, January.

31. Ibid.

32. Subramanyam, M. (1975) 'On the optimality of international capital market integration', Journal of Financial Economics, 2.

33. Narpati, B. (1976) 'Financial markets in the EEC', Common Market, vol. 7, no. 1.

34. Williams, D. (1965) 'The development of capital markets in Europe', International Monetary Fund Staff Paper, xii, March.

35. The European Economic Community Commission (1966) 'The development of a European capital market', report by a group of experts under the direction of C. Segre, Brussels, November, p. 311.

36. Ibid. p. 238.

37. Ibid. p. 243.

38. Ibid. p. 245.

39. Ibid. p. 213.

40. Warehame, W. (1972) 'The supervision and regulation of security markets in the EEC', paper presented at a Conference on 'The integration of European securities markets', organised by the London Stock Exchange, Brussels, October 11.

41. Ibid.

42. Hessels, J. (1983) 'Prospects and problems of integrated securities markets', Euromoney, March.

43. Cohen, M. (1971) 'A large capital market: the American experience', paper presented at a Conference on 'The integration of European securities markets', organised by L'Université Internationale des Sciences, Luxembourg, 19-20 November.

Chapter Two

STOCK MARKETS IN THE ARAB GULF COUNTRIES

I   THE KUWAITI STOCK MARKET

A   Historical background (1960-1980)

Following the second world war, increases in oil production and exports resulted in a rapid growth of Kuwaiti's financial resources, which in turn helped in the establishment of a Kuwaiti financial market. The Kuwaiti economic activities, such as trade, fishing, boat building and pearling, which took place in the pre-oil era, were limited in terms of ownership capital, and technical requirements. Therefore, after the major oil discoveries in 1937, a branch of the British Bank of the Middle East was established in 1941, thus signalling the birth of the Kuwaiti financial sector.

The historical development of the Kuwaiti stock market may be divided into three main sections, as follows:

(1) **Transitional period from the traditional to the oil economy (second world war until 1960):** During this period, public shareholding companies were formed and corporate equity issues represented the first type of tradeable securities in the Kuwaiti economy. This period also saw the incorporation of four Kuwaiti shareholding companies - the National Bank of Kuwait (1952), the Kuwait National Cinema Company (1954), Kuwait National Airways (1956), and the Kuwait Oil Tankers Company (1960). The cumulative capital of these companies amounted to about KD 13,857,708 million, with issue shares totalling over one million, thus representing about 1.9 per cent of oil revenues

for this period and 8.7 per cent of the value of land acquisitions'. (1) These issued shares were so small in size, and shareholders had such a narrow base, that any meaningful stock trading was not possible. In addition, companies' assets grew so rapidly and their profits reached such a scale that share ownership was seen as a very profitable investment. Investors concentrated their activities in the real estate market because it offered huge opportunities for rapid profits. The government took advantage of this and introduced construction and land acquisition programmes which, because they generated a great demand for land, resulted in a rapid increase in land prices. Therefore, during this period the main form of wealth holding was land and real estate, constituting a huge proportion of the capital funds which the government had transferred to the private sector.

(2) **The building up of the stock market (1960-1970):** This period can be further divided into two sub-periods. In the first period, between 1960 and 1962, the newly formed shareholding companies and the issue of public shares were further expanded; in the second, between 1963 and 1970, there existed a relative recession in both new stock issues and dealings in existing stocks.

Between 1960 and 1962, the shareholding companies' sector emerged as the most important sector in the Kuwaiti economy. The stock market developed its economic and financial activities in such a way as to become one of the major fields of economic activity in the country. When the commercial companies law was brought into effect in May 1960, the newly created shareholding companies gained a new impetus and 13 new public shareholding companies were established with a capital totalling KD 35.8 million. The government played an active role in the establishment and promotion of shareholding companies. It participated in seven out of the 13 companies with capital of KD 15.4 million, that is, 43 per cent of the companies' total capital, while the total paid-up capital 'amounted to KD 20 million or about 55 per cent of the total capital of the new companies'. (2) Although during this short period the volume of capital inflow into the shareholding companies sector multiplied, the funds that these established companies absorbed amounted to a small proportion of private sector investable funds. The large expansion in the share's issue base came with the establishment of new companies and the increase in the capital of existing ones. Between 1959 and 1962 the volume of issued shares rose from 0.985 million to 5.3 million with 3.6 million in private sector hands.

Between 1963 and 1970, the growth of the shareholding companies' sector continued at a slower rate, with only eight public and two closed shareholding companies being incorporated. Also, trading activities showed a marked slackening, while stock prices declined. The cumulative capital of these companies amounted to KD 43.75 million with government participation of KD 26.3 million. The number of shareholding companies continued to increase until it reached 25 per cent at the end of 1968, with a total capital of KD 100 million of which 43 per cent were government shares and 57 per cent for the private sector. The continuous decline in the stock prices reached its peak in 1967.

(3) **1970–1980:** During this period, the change that took place in the stock market led to an increase in its capacity to absorb and circulate funds. Among these developments was the issuing of a number of laws and resolutions which constituted the foundation for the trading operations of Kuwaiti shareholding companies, and which in turn was the first step for the emergence of the stock exchange. These developments made the role of the stock market in Kuwaiti economic life an important one and were able to create changes in individual attitudes and tendencies towards financial and economic activities.

During this period, the development which took place in the local share market in 1977 led to the introduction of a number of decisions and regulations to check any further establishment of public shareholding companies in Kuwait. Therefore, some financiers had to turn to neighbouring Gulf countries such as Bahrain and the United Arab Emirates, whose laws encouraged the establishment of such companies. A large number of Gulf shareholding companies, now numbering 35, were set up in 1976, 1979 and 1980 respectively, with the capital shares offered for trading amounting to KD 3,500 millions, more than the shares of Kuwaiti public shareholding companies which did not exceed KD 837 million. The important factors behind the establishment of Gulf companies were the following:

(1) the narrow local market and its inability to absorb local capital;
(2) local capital faced economic risks such as inflation, stagnation and exchange rate fluctuations, because of its small size;
(3) local policies of limiting public companies.

Because it was Kuwaiti initiative and capital which made possible the formation of these Gulf companies, trading in the shares of these companies in Kuwait was done on a large scale. However, such trading 'did not take place in the official stock exchange, but in an official parallel market, the Al-Manakh market, where groups of brokers promoted these shares and facilitated trading therein'. (3)

B. **Development (1980–1986)**

During the early 1980s the securities market in Kuwait went through various changes and moved towards a new dimension, that of channelling domestic capital towards the establishment of Gulf joint stock companies. Dealers became interested in trading in the shares of these companies and securities trading markets came into being - one official and with rules and regulations, the other non-official and known as Al Manakh market.

In the 1980s considerations were again given to the construction of a new building for the brokers and their businesses to give official status for the new market in Gulf company shares. Steps were also taken to organise the management and control of the market in a more formal manner than was previously used. The government also saw the need to establish the Kuwaiti stock exchange as an organised body. Legislation was drafted to establish an independent public corporation with its own governing body, with the Minister of Commerce as chairman of its board of management. The board would also be given the 'financial autonomy and the authority to levy fees and charges sufficient to provide it with an adequate source of revenue for its own needs'. (4) However, all these attempts during the 1980s to regulate the stock market within a definite framework did not materialise and were merely words on paper.

During 1981, apart from Kuwaiti public joint stock companies, two new types of joint stock companies were approved and included in the local stock exchange - the Kuwaiti Closed Joint Stock Companies and the Gulf Joint Stock Companies.

Kuwaiti public joint stock companies
By December 1981, Kuwaiti joint stock companies numbered 39 with a total capital of KD 621 million. Because of speculation in the local market, the prices of the shares of these companies increased greatly despite the recent establishment of these companies.

Kuwaiti closed joint stock companies
In 1981, and for the first time, the authorities opened the market for the Kuwaiti closed joint stock companies to offer their shares to the public in the stock exchange under certain conditions which we will consider later. By the end of December, six companies were allowed to put their shares to the public with a total capital of KD 51 million. Specific conditions for trading in these shares were set up by the Ministry of Commerce and Industry:

(1) The company should have a capital of no less than KD 5 million.
(2) The company should have been in operation for at least five years and should have accumulated profits for its operations in the last two years.
(3) The founders of the new company are not permitted to dispose of their shares until two years have elapsed since the date of registration.
(4) Any closed company thinking of trading its shares in the stock exchange should submit a detailed financial report on its activities and a balance sheet in at least two daily newspapers.

Gulf joint stock companies
The market for Gulf shares grew in importance in 1981 when the authorities put forward certain conditions to allow these shares to be quoted in the local stock exchange (secondary market). Dealing in the shares of Gulf companies became important because of the 'abundance of national funds seeking viable investment opportunities within the Kuwaiti economy, which is characterised by a limited absorptive

23

capacity - combined with the instability and crisis involving foreign investment outlets'. (5) During that year, two of the companies - Gulf Real Estate Investment Company and Gulf Agricultural Development Company - were registered with a total share trading amounting to 33 million. However, unofficial trade in shares of Gulf companies in the local market did not stop, for several reasons. The heavy activity of the shares of Gulf companies demanded the setting up of local offices to conduct transactions.

Until 1981, trading in the shares of Gulf companies was concluded in an authorised way without any official framework. In a further attempt to regulate Kuwait's stock market, 'whereby conditions were set for such companies to officially offer their shares after listing them in the Kuwait stock exchange along with the shares of Kuwaiti public joint stock companies', (6) the Ministry of Commerce and Industry issued new listing rules:

(1) To be considered official, a company must be set up in a Gulf state which has signed an economic agreement amongst the Gulf states of which Kuwait is a member.
(2) The decree applies only to those companies set up as of the date of the decree.
(3) The founders' shares should be excluded from the issued capital of the company or retained by the founders for a period of three years.
(4) The shareholders of the company must carry a Gulf state citizenship or membership of institutions incorporated therein.
(5) To become eligible for official listing, the companies should have been established for at least three years and should have had a profit record of no less than ten per cent of their nominal capital (minimum of KD 5 m) in the past two years.
(6) The companies have to keep their activities within the purpose put forward by the association and only revenue derived from this activity will be allowed when computing their profit record.
(7) For a period of three years from the date of admission, the companies must promise not to increase their capital in any way other than free bonus.
(8) The companies must also promise to establish no subsidiary companies where they hold 25 per cent or more of the capital within the following five years.

Another attempt to regulate the Gulf shares market was initiated by the Ministry of Commerce and Industry which set up an ad hoc consultative committee with four representatives of the Gulf companies, two experts, a representative of the chamber of commerce and industry, a representative of the Ministry of Finance and two representatives of the Ministry of Commerce and Industry. The committee put forward the following points:

(1) Proposals should be drawn to regulate and control trading in Gulf shares.

(2) All matters relating to capital adjustment of any company or changes in, or additions to, its objectives should be regulated.

(3) Matters proposed by the Ministry of Commerce and Industry, through its chairman, in respect of Gulf companies should be considered.

The securities markets (both the official stock market and the parallel or unofficial Al-Manakh) witnessed many developments in 1982 of which the parallel market is the most important for our discussion because of its implications on the Kuwaiti economy in general, and the official market in particular. As we have seen, the establishment of Gulf companies by Kuwaiti initiative and capital made the Kuwaiti dealers conduct their trade in an unofficial parallel market, the Al-Manakh market. Trading in the shares of these companies brought sharp rises in prices. Also, in the absence of proper control and supervision, the dealers acted irresponsibly, thus giving rise to a sharp crisis which was basically the result of forward transactions. 'The signs of the crisis emerged in September 1982 when trading in the Al-Manakh market sagged suddenly to 72 million shares against 602 million in the previous month.' (7) This sudden development in the activity of the Al-Manakh made it clear to the dealers, traders and observers that the already expected negative consequences in this market had come true, 'leading a number of them to fail to pay the value of their cheques related to the heavy forward sales and transactions they had concluded, while many dealers in the market failed to discharge their financial commitments'. (8) Several traders terminated payment of their cheques thus causing the Al-Manakh crisis.

The factors which contributed to the evolution and harshness of the Al-Manakh crisis were the following:

(1) The surge of forward cheques involving huge amounts exceeding the financial resources of the traders which came from the irrational optimism which took place in the market in the previous two years.

(2) The heavy demand for shares resulted in the transactions reaching a ridiculous price to a level inconsistent with the value of the profits distributed. Some speculators used the shares acquired through such transactions to finance their dealings, which were then used to finance further unlimited transactions and speculation.

(3) The establishment of closed companies and joint ventures by some financiers facilitated cash transactions which resulted in liquidity developments as it enabled them to obtain large quantities of shares at low cost and then offer them in the market at high prices. The establishment of such closed companies was made possible because of the ease of their legal formalisation when compared to public-subscription shareholding companies and because the public willingly bought their shares which made those companies similar to the public subscription companies.

(4) The fact that trading in the parallel market lacked the existence of laws and regulatory measures which prompted people to speculate in an attempt to make vast gains within a short time, 'irrespective of the productivity of the companies or their real financial position'. (9)

These irregularities in the Al-Manakh market have affected the official market stock exchange to a great extent.

The negative effects resulting from the unusual developments in the Al-Manakh market were not confined to drops in the volume of trading and share prices, or the failure of dealers to repay their debts, but also extended to the efficiency of the Kuwaiti securities market, especially the absence of 'market makers' who had dominated its activity and steered its movement. (10)

Stock exchange activities slowed down considerably, so that

the role of the Kuwaiti securities market to absorb and make rational the capital funds and to manage them soundly was challenged. It prevented the establishment of company control, and allowed speculation which resulted in disorderly fluctuations in share prices 'thus rendering the prices inexpressive of the real financial position of the companies and liable to limit the diversification and effectiveness of others tools in the securities market'. (11)

During 1983 the securities market witnessed a number of regulatory developments and measures for the Al-Manakh market. The government issued legal measures during 1983 intended to contain the economic developments arising from the post-dated cheques to defend the rights of small investors.

Among the most important laws and decisions was the fixing of the maximum capital payable to creditors through the trust fund. Any amounts up to KD 25 thousand were to be paid in cash and the balance in the form of bonds with a maturity range of six months to six years. Another was the establishment of the Forward Shares Transaction Settlement Corporation in April 1983, to undertake the settlement of transactions and evaluate the assets of persons referred to the Corporation. The Corporation was also legally authorised to manage, liquidate and execute settlements, and act on the behalf of creditors whose debts resulted from forward share transactions.

A number of the suggestions and solutions presented in 1982 and 1983 for the solution of the Al-Manakh crisis 'focused on the need to reduce the total debt to a reasonable ratio above the spot prices'. (12)

As for the stock exchange, the authorities issued a decree on 14 August 1983 to regulate the Kuwaiti securities market. Management of the market was given to an independent committee with the Minister of Commerce and Industry as its chairman and consisting of other members selected from different Ministries. The committee's job was to deal with the application of rules to regulate financial papers in the market and supervise transactions covering such papers. Its job was also to act in accordance with the laws against dubious transactions; to take a decision on the applications submitted for the registration of brokers, shares of Kuwaiti shareholding companies and other financial papers; and in cases of emergency, put a temporary stop to deals in the market or in the shares of companies.

The committee was also decreed to help the market follow and analyse the prices of shares and bonds that were listed in the market; evaluate forward transactions and the relation between them and spot sales; and to analyse and publish the data relative to the market, traded financial papers and listed companies. The decree limited membership in the market to Kuwaiti companies which placed their shares for public subscription; closed Kuwaiti shareholding companies which the committee approved for membership; brokers of financial papers in the market.

Other by-laws were issued on 7 November 1983 dealing with a number of subjects, such as the market's objectives, management and membership; the registration, acceptance and negotiation of financial papers; the budget, disputes, arbitration and discipline. The by-laws also set the conditions to be satisfied by any company licensed to engage in brokerage business, which included the following:

(1) The company and all partners must be Kuwaitis.

(2) The brokers must be Kuwaitis with good qualifications, experienced and trained in accordance with what the committee sees fit; and having good reputation.

(3) Those on the management side should not have any previous prison sentence or have been declared bankrupt.

(4) The market committee fixes the amount of paid-up capital after the submission of a bank guarantee.

During 1984, the securities market witnessed a number of new regulations and measures, in addition to the opening of the new stock exchange buildings and the application of the system of written bidding in trading transactions.

One law concerning the disposition of joint stock company shares and financial papers aimed at recognising the legitimacy of the disposition of joint stock company shares and of tradings covering the unlicensed Gulf shares.

Another law concerning the rules and regulations governing share trading in the market covered a number of matters. The market management must indicate the times and places for the conduct of transactions related to financial papers. They also adopted the method of 'written bidding' in trade where the broker had to put down on a special board the information relative to the transactions he planned to conduct. The market management then supervised the dealing arrangements.

Still another law was the Ministerial decision concerning the preparation and submission of company closing accounts for 1984. This decision was taken following the outcome of the Al-Manakh market crisis to define the accounting procedures to be applied by companies in preparing their balance sheets, as follows:

(1) Post-dated cheques drawn on non-referred persons and until settlement should be approved at their value. When settled amicably, and involving settlements approved by the arbitration authorities, they should be endorsed at the value of such settlements. Post-dated cheques related to forward share transactions and drawn on referred persons, the value of whose dinars have been assessed, should be endorsed at the dinar-value as set by the official authorities. Bonds issued by the trust fund should be endorsed at the current value.

(2) Investments in the shares of Kuwaiti and Gulf companies should be evaluated at the total cost or the total market value. The Kuwaiti securities market issues a list to determine the share market value on the date of the balance sheet. On the other hand, investments in the shares of those companies which are registered with the Kuwaiti securities market should be evaluated either at cost or at the value given in the market. Those not registered should be evaluated either at cost or at the book value given in the 1983 financial statements.

During 1986, the securities market witnessed a number of new regulations and measures to help channel savings towards profitable investments. The first of these strategies was to make the local market concentrate on placating the rate of share turnover and restraining speculation. In addition, securities were to be held as long as possible, for investment and not speculative reasons. It was argued that such an increase in demands for securities would be met through increasing the capital of the companies by issuing new shares for public subscription or by establishing new shareholding companies, which in turn would channel domestic savings towards real investment.

The second strategy was the installation by the Ministry

of Finance of a new set of rules to work the new exchange. The first rule gave the supervision of the management of the new stock exchange to a committee which included the Minister of Finance, representatives of the chamber of commerce, the central bank and stock brokers. The second rule was that bids must be made in writing.

The third concerned avoiding wide price fluctuations by dividing groups of shares into units of 500 to 100,000 shares. The fourth gave the authorities of the stock exchange the right to examine the financial position of the companies listed. The fifth stipulated that the stock exchange would list 39 public shareholding companies and 7 closed companies and that an official parallel market would be created on the main floor which would list 30 Gulf companies. The sixth made the companies listed on the exchange pay an annual fee of KD 10,000 plus 0.001 per cent of their capital. The seventh forbade the ownership of stockbroking firms by individuals and stipulated that stockbroking companies must have a minimum capital of KD 100,000 and provide a deposit of KD 250,000 as security against malpractice. The eight licensed eleven stockbroking firms and included training sessions of 16 weeks for employees on trading and financial knowledge. The ninth allowed only two companies to act as market makers. And the tenth admitted Kuwaiti dinar bonds for listing on the exchange.

In addition to those developments, the Central Bank of Kuwait reviewed the financial standing of 79 money changing establishments and 38 investment companies. In October 1985, trading in Gulf shares was suspended by the government until an assessment of their values was made. Some 33 Gulf companies listed on the new official parallel market were reviewed by the central bank which advised the liquidation of four, the merging of another four, changing boards of directors of eleven, and changing the executive managements of ten. In addition, 62 closed companies were also reviewed and asked for, closing three, liquidating 25 and merging five.

The securities market in Kuwait witnessed several developments in 1986 which were associated with many regulatory rules and decisions, all of which accelerated market activity. Of the actions, the authorities adopted regulatory measures towards Gulf joint stock companies, fixing the share price for each company according to the value of its assets, which in turn led to the suspension of trade in the shares of these companies. The regulatory measures led to the liquidation of 25 closed companies and the merger of another eight. As for public shareholding companies, three companies were liquidated in 1986. To improve companies' financial positions and productivity, they secured management and extended support, promoted the productivity and provided customs protection against competitive products.

Supervision of the securities market was intensified during 1986. A price unit system was set to soften the speculation. This provided that price increments during the trading session should not exceed five points. A share brokerage list was issued specifying brokerage commission to be based on the share value of any company concluded within a day, while market commission was determined as equal to 30 per cent of the commissions. In addition, terms were issued to regulate the brokerage profession in the market. One of the conditions provided that the applicant should be a partner or an employee of one of the registered brokerage companies and should pass all theoretical and practical examinations.

Several rules for regulating the market's activities were issued by the authorities. One of these was decision no. 5 on the rules governing the sale of forward shares. This entitled the management to specify the brokerage companies through which forward shares might be traded and provided that the differential between the price of a forward transaction and its spot price should not exceed 25 per cent of the total value of transaction. Decision no. 16 on the listing and regulating of the work of market makers stipulated that a company should be shareholding or a Kuwaiti financial institution and its paid-up capital should not be less than KD 10m. Also, the company must have financial, technical and administrative capabilities to carry out this type of activity. The decision also specified the trading period of market makers after which they were not allowed to trade in shares among one another, unless through a registered broker.

A third rule was decision no. 132 which amended the provisions of the commercial companies law. The first amendment reduced the minimum par value of shares which offered new channels for demand of domestic financial papers; this had made the sector a strong competitor to other sectors of Kuwaiti companies due to the high values of shares compared with non-Kuwaiti companies. The second amendment reduced the procedures of share title transfer. Transactions are now being entered in the register available in the market hall provided that the market management furnishes the company with data relating to transactions concluded on its shares. This new procedure will speed up conclusion of transactions. A third amendment gave the shareholding company the right to buy its shares which do not exceed 10 per cent of the total and stipulated that buying shares should not be financed from the company's funds.

A fourth decree regulated the procedures of securities trading settlements and the clearing room at the Kuwait Securities Market. Applying the clearing system will minimise complicated procedures such as title transfer, debt settlement and so on. The clearing room is entitled to retain the securities registered with and acceptable by the market for their owners, to be delivered when they prove their ownership. The application of the clearing system obligates traders and brokers to meet their obligation and be disciplined.

C   Activities (1980–1986)

This part of the book will discuss in detail the major developments and changes which took place in the official stock market during the period 1980-86, in terms of issue base, price and value and volume of trading.

Issue base

Shares issued by the Kuwaiti public-subscription joint stock companies by the end of 1985 totalled around 1.1 billion compared with 1067 million in 1984, 1 billion in 1983, 837 million in 1982, 621 million in 1981, and 165 million in 1980.

By the end of 1985, total government share within the total share issue rose to 57 per cent against 52 per cent in 1984, 49 per cent in 1983, 36 per cent in 1982, 38 per cent in 1981 and 34 per cent in 1980. The expansion in the issue base was a result of the establishment in 1984 of new public joint stock companies and the issuing of new shares in the form of bonds shares, both free of charge and at a premium.

In 1985 the bonus shares totalled 8.3 million shares and the premium shares totalled 18.9 million. In 1984 the bonus shares totalled 29.6 million shares, in addition to 34.1

million new shares issued at a premium. While in 1983, the distribution of profits was limited to free bonus shares distributed among shareholders and totalling KD 147 million without issuing any new shares at premium. On the other hand, in 1982 the expansion of shares was distributed among new companies (50 million), free bonus shares (95.4 million), and at premium shares (66.3 million). The free bonus shares issued in 1981 totalled 41.9 million, while the shares issued at premium totalled 38.4 million. This compares with 35 million free bonus shares and 26 million shares at premium in 1980.

The base shares were distributed among several local shareholding companies in the following manner. The financial companies constituting the banking, investment and insurance sectors always came first in the years 1981, 1982 and 1983 with a percentage of 40 per cent, 40 per cent and 41 per cent respectively. While the industrial companies took second place in the same years, comprising 37 per cent, 30 per cent and 32 per cent respectively. The real estate sector came third, having 10 per cent in 1980, 13 per cent in 1981, 15 per cent in 1983 and 3 per cent in 1984.

Volume and value of trading
Data available on share trading in the local stock exchange for the period 1980-86 covered shares of 48 companies divided into three groups: the Kuwaiti public-subscription shareholding companies (39), the Kuwaiti closed shareholding companies (7), and the Gulf shareholding companies (2). Here, we will concentrate on the Kuwaiti public-subscription shareholding companies in accordance with the weight they carry in the economy. The other two companies will be referred to briefly.

During this period, 1980 saw a drop of 27.9 per cent and 14.8 per cent in the overall value and volume of traded shares compared with the previous year. The volume of traded shares totalled 144.7 million, to the value of KD 1325.5 million as against 169 million in 1979 to the value of KD 1837 million. The decline in trading volume was more pronounced in the shares of insurance companies, banks and industrial companies which dropped by 70 per cent, 41 per cent and 34 per cent respectively. 1981 witnessed a record volume of trading in 246.8 million shares, while the total value of dealings amounted to KD 1949.8 million. Here, the trading volume of the real estate companies ranked first at

Table 2.1: Kuwaiti shareholding companies - public subscription: volume of traded shares in 1980-1986

Sectors	Volume (million shares)								
	1980	1981	%	1981	1982	%	1982	1983	%
Banks	47.7	30.5	-36	30.5	33.6	10.2	33.6	12.9	-61.6
Investment	24.5	42.8	75	42.8	35.6	-40.2	35.6	10.2	-60.2
Insurance	1.1	1.4	27	1.4	3.9	178.6	3.9	1.8	-53.8
Industrial	14.8	40.5	174	40.5	39.0	-3.7	39.0	16.2	-58.5
Transport	23.6	34.0	44	34.0	9.4	-72.4	9.4	3.3	-65.0
Services	9.3	47.8	414	47.8	10.6	-77.8	10.6	5.1	-51.9
Realty	22.7	49.8	119	49.8	61.8	24.1	61.8	11.9	-80.7
Total	144.7	246.8	72	246.8	183.9	-25.5	183.9	61.4	-66.6

	1983	1984	%	1984	1985	%	1985	1986	%
Banks	12.9	8.4	-35	8.4	18.9	125.0	18.9	50.1	165.1
Investment	10.2	1.3	-87	1.3	0.8	-38.5	0.8	4.4	450.0
Insurance	1.8	0.1	-94	0.1	0.2	100.0	0.2	0.8	300.0
Industrial	16.2	2.3	-86	2.3	5.9	156.5	5.9	26.0	340.7
Transport	3.3	0.4	-88	0.4	–	–	–	–	–
Services	5.1	2.8	-45	2.8	11.2	300.0	11.2	41.9	274.0
Realty	11.9	4.5	-62	4.5	3.8	-15.5	3.8	20.9	450.0
Total	16.4	19.8	-68	19.8	40.8	106.0	40.8	144.1	253.2

Source: Kuwaiti Stock Exchange, Annual Statistics, various issues

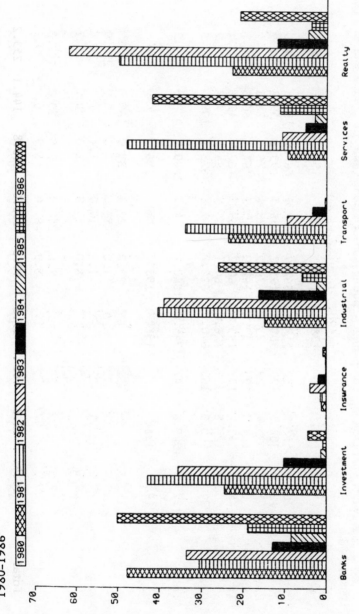

Figure 2.1: Kuwaiti shareholding companies – public subscription: volume of traded shares in 1980–1986

Table 2.2: Kuwaiti shareholding companies – public subscription: value of traded shares in 1980–1986

Volume (million shares)

Sectors	1980	1981	%	1982	%	1983	%
Banks	765.2	517.7	-32	667.9	29.0	183.8	-72.5
Investment	138.5	308.5	123	195.8	-36.5	59.8	-69.5
Insurance	18.2	23.4	29	76.5	28.4	28.8	-62.4
Industrial	47.3	139.3	195	167.0	19.9	66.6	-60.1
Transport	81.2	193.8	139	60.2	-69.6	12.6	-79.1
Services	30.4	126.8	317	64.1	-49.4	17.8	-72.2
Realty	244.7	640.3	162	628.7	-1.8	109.5	-82.6
Total	1325.5	1949.8	47	1860.2	-4.8	478.9	-74.3

Sectors	1983	1984	%	1985	%	1986	%
Banks	183.8	69	-62	83.0	20.3	165.0	98.8
Investment	59.8	5	-92	1.0	-80.0	3.0	200.0
Insurance	28.8	1	-97	1.1	10.0	1.5	36.4
Industrial	66.6	7	-90	8.0	14.3	0.7	-91.2
Transport	12.6	1	-92	-	-	-	-
Services	17.8	2	-89	7.0	250.0	20.5	192.8
Realty	109.5	27	-75	8.9	-67.0	10.7	20.2
Total	478.9	112	-77	109.0	-2.7	201.4	84.8

Source: Kuwaiti Stock Exchange, Annual Statistics, various issues

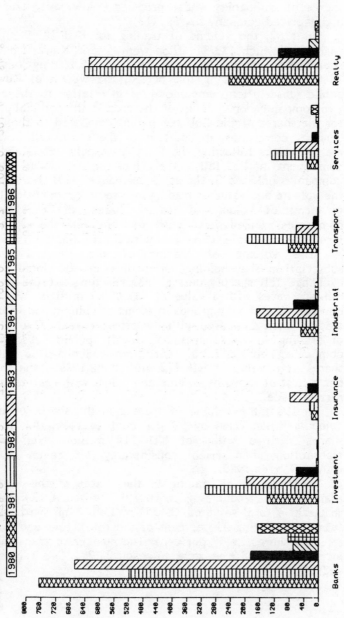

Figure 2.2: Kuwaiti shareholding companies - public subscription: value of traded shares (in million dinars) in 1980-1986

1980 1981 1982 1983 1984 1985 1986

Banks   Investment   Insurance   Industrial   Transport   Services   Realty

49.8 million, while the banks came last at 30.5 million 'a fact reflecting preference on the dealers for trading in shares of companies whose prices are low, over trade in highly priced company shares'. (13)

In 1982, the volume of trading totalled 183.9 million shares, of which 183.9 million went to the Kuwaiti public-subscription companies while its value of trading was KD 1860.2 million. During this period, the weight of Kuwaiti public-subscription companies rose in relation to the other two companies 'on account of the drop in the nominal prices for the shares of the Gulf companies compared to those for Kuwaiti companies, in addition to the sharp fall in their market prices following the Souq Al-Manakh crisis and the consequent market fall in the prices for the shares of Gulf companies unlisted in the stock exchange'. (14) If we break the volume and value of trading into sectors, we notice that, in terms of volume of traded shares, the real estate companies ranked first with 61.8 million shares, while insurance companies came last with 3.9 million.

The volume of trading of the Kuwaiti public subscription shareholding companies in the local stock exchange fell sharply during 1983 reaching a total of 61.4 million shares with a value of KD 478.9 million. The drop covered all company groups in terms of volume and value of trading when compared with the previous year. The volume of trading in the shares of Kuwaiti public subscription companies kept on falling until they reached 19.8 million shares at a value of KD 112 million in 1984. Bank shares came first in terms of volume and value, with real estate in second place.

In 1985, the volume of trading in the shares of these companies had risen by 98 per cent to reach 42 million shares with a value of KD 112 million. Number of transactions had risen considerably to reach 10,310 transactions in 1985.

The volume of trading in the shares of the Kuwaiti shareholding companies grew in 1986 to reach 123 million shares at a total value of KD 354 million. Bank shares came first, constituting 41 per cent of the total, followed by the services shares at 34 per cent. The number of transactions increased by 122.9 per cent to reach 23,000. See Tables 2.1 and 2.2.

Prices

The index for Kuwaiti joint stock companies shows that while in 1980 no remarkable change had occurred, significant annual rises in 1981 and 1982 - 56 per cent and 4 per cent respectively - and a decline of 10 per cent in 1983 became noticeable.

During 1980, an 18 per cent increase in the price level was noticed in the second quarter to show a decline of 2 per cent and 6.6 per cent in the third and fourth quarters. 'This is attributed to a number of factors some of which are related to the war between Iraq and Iran and some to the accelerated levels of international interest rates, especially on the US dollar.' (15) Those companies whose levels of prices declined were insurance companies, industrial companies, investment companies and banks; others, such as services companies, transport companies and real estate companies, witnessed an increase in their prices. The prices of shares in the local market also fluctuated for several reasons - distribution of share dividends, economic and international conditions and crises, and motives of speculation.

The rise in the share price index for Kuwaiti joint stock companies in 1981 was a result of the sharp increases in the share price index of all companies, but particularly transport companies (113 per cent), real estate (71 per cent), investment companies (70 per cent) and banks (55 per cent). 'Speculation, together with the distribution of free bonus shares and new share issues, played a significant role in pushing the prices upwards.' (16)

At the end of 1982, the Kuwaiti public subscription companies showed a slight increase of 4 per cent with the bank group having the highest rate in share price increases (18 per cent) followed by the investment companies (14 per cent) and insurance and transport companies (9 per cent).

In 1983 the price index for shares traded in the stock exchange decreased around 10 per cent with only the investment companies registering a price rise of 1 per cent.

The prices of these shares further fell during 1984; insurance companies dropped by 59 per cent, banks by 51 per cent and transport by 50 per cent.

In 1985 the price index of shares traded in the stock exchange reached 29.45, while banks reached 43.83, insurance companies fell by 47.9 per cent.

An increase was witnessed in 1986 in the share price index where the service sector reached 49.2 per cent and

Table 2.3: Kuwaiti shareholding companies – public subscription: share price index 1980-1986

(January 1976 = 100)

Sectors	1980	1981	%	1982	%	1983	%	1984	%	1985	%	1986	%
Banks	468	729	55	862	18	727	-16	354	-51	318	-10.2	421	32.4
Investment	242	412	70	470	14	475	1	196	-59	36	-81.6	162	350.0
Insurance	694	813	17	885	9	812	-8	336	-59	240	-28.6	394	64.2
Industrial	212	298	41	301	1	296	-2	172	-42	111	-35.5	44	-60.4
Transport	140	298	113	325	9	256	-21	128	-50	-	-	-	-
Services	359	498	39	488	-2	411	-16	240	-42	31	-87.1	10	-67.7
Realty	465	794	71	810	2	613	-24	374	-39	182	-51.3	164	-9.9
General Index	313	490	56	509	4	461	-10	239	-48	153	-35.9	199	30.1

Source: Kuwaiti Stock Exchange, Annual Statistics, various issues

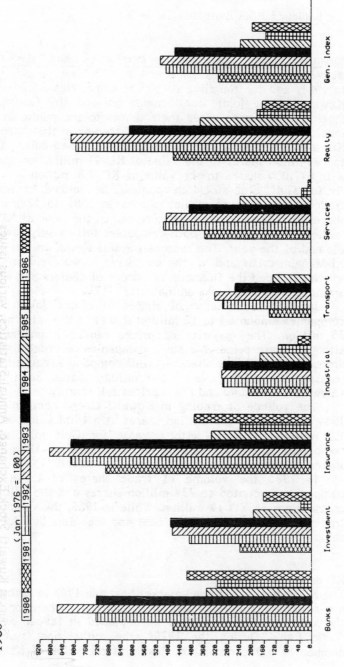

Figure 2.3: Kuwaiti shareholding companies - public subscription: share price index in 1980-1986

(Jan 1976 = 100)

1980 1981 1982 1983 1984 1985 1986

Banks   Investment   Insurance   Industrial   Transport   Services   Realty   Gen. Index

920
880
840
800
760
720
680
640
600
560
520
480
440
400
360
320
280
240
200
160
120
80
40
0

41

the banks 23.5 per cent (see Table 2.3).

Kuwaiti closed shareholding companies and the Gulf shareholding companies

In 1981, and for the first time, the authorities allowed the Kuwaiti closed joint stock companies and the Gulf joint stock companies to offer their shares to the public in the local stock exchange. The volume of trading in the shares of Kuwaiti closed joint stock companies increased during 1982 to 14 million shares to the value of KD 41 million compared with 677,000 shares to the value of KD 2.8 million in 1981. As for Gulf joint stock companies, the volume of shares traded rose from 33 million shares in 1981 to 57 million shares in 1982 while their value remained the same at KD 37 million. Share prices of both companies fell sharply towards the end of the year. The reasons for this slowdown were the Al-Manakh crisis and '... the excessive forward share sales which exceeded the financial resources of dealers and which precipitated bottlenecks on maturity'. (17)

In 1983 the volume of shares of closed joint stock companies amounted to 12 million shares to the value of KD 33 million. The majority of prices remained unchanged, although share prices for some companies recorded limited drops. Dealings in the shares of Gulf companies reached four transactions which covered one million shares, to a total value of KD 116,000 and share prices fell sharply.

The volume of trading in Kuwaiti closed companies in 1984 amounted to 1.5 million shares at a total value of KD 1.6 million compared with a value for Gulf joint stock companies of KD 2.7 million and a volume of 49 million shares.

In 1985 the volume of trade shares of these two companies amounted to 734 million shares and the value of transactions to KD 14 million. While in 1986, the volume of trading increased by 28.4 per cent and the value by 88.2 per cent.

KD denominated bonds

The KD denominated bond market began in 1968 in favour of non-residents from Arab and other companies when bonds to the value of KD 15 million were placed in favour of the World Bank. During the 1970s, the authorities issued a number of KD denominated bonds to the value of KD 589 million of which KD 45 million (five issues) favoured local borrowers and KD 543.8 million (66 issues) foreign borrowers.

Such issues were induced by the stability of the Kuwaiti dinar exchange rate as well as the expertise gained by some Kuwaiti investment companies in the field of management and underwriting, which in turn encouraged prime borrowers to enter the KD denominated bond market. (18)

During the early 1980s, in the primary market for KD bonds, 20 issues were made to the value of KD 134 million, with an interest higher than 10 per cent per annum, covering residents and non-residents. Of these KD bonds, one issue to the value of KD 7 million was issued in 1982, five new issues totalling KD 34 million in 1981, eight issues to the value of KD 53 million in 1980, as against five issues to the value of KD 27 million in 1983 and three issues in the amount of KD 24 million in 1984. As a result, bonds issued in the primary market between 1968 and 1983 totalled 86 issues to the value of KD 669.8 million. Some of these issues carried a fluctuating interest rate equal to 0.025 per cent above the average interest rate on local inter-bank deposits. New issues were in favour of local borrowers after the central bank issued a decision suspending KD bond issues in favour of non-residents.

The year 1985 witnessed a sluggish trading in the KD denominated bond market and only 28 issues were set down for trading to a value of KD 197 million. This trend continued into 1986 when the total value of traded shares amounted to KD 275,000 distributed among 13 transactions only. This was because borrowers resorting to buying these bonds with relatively high interest.

As for the secondary market, trading in KD denominated bonds was limited from the time they were issued up to 1977, as companies which specialised in crediting an active secondary market for these bonds were non-existent. In April 1977, the Arab company for trading securities, which was established as a Kuwait joint stock company, gave the secondary market for these bonds a new push which remained inadequate because of marketing problems resulting from uncertainties in the international markets, most important of which was the rise of interest rates. Another important event was that the local issues and the secondary market for KD denominated bonds remained stagnant in 1979 and 1980 because domestic markets lacked the administrative and financial abilities to keep pace with the favourable developments in international financial markets. Nevertheless, the secondary market for KD denominated bonds witnessed some activity during the first years of the 1980s, with trading in bonds totalling KD 144 million in 1983, or 20 per cent of the total bonds placed in the market.

D   **Methods of Dealing**

Methods of dealing on the Kuwaiti market reflect the society within which they are based. As Kuwait is socially a compact and close-knit society, where everyone - especially the wealthy merchant community - is known to everyone else, the system of dealing in the market is conducted on a client-to-client basis, 'with the broker acting as no more than a record-keeper and referee'. (19) Licensed stockbrokers have no monopoly on arranging deals. Deals are sometimes concluded in the broker's office or privately by two clients who meet face-to-face when agreeing on a transaction. Investors are not obliged to employ a broker when dealing if they find it easier to deal among their acquaintances. Of course, brokers are sometimes employed by the client to find a buyer; nevertheless, the final contract is regarded as being between two clients and brokers regard themselves as absolved from any responsibility for seeing that settlement is duly completed as is the normal practice elsewhere. In this system shares are rarely offered openly on the market.

Because a deal is conducted between two identified persons, the seller takes his share certificate and the broker's contract note to the company registrar where he gets a receipt. On the second day of the deal, the seller gives the receipt to the buyer and receives a cheque. In return, the buyer gives his copy of the contract to the company where he 'received a temporary note of title pending issue of the formal share certificate'. (20) In such a system, the broker does not guarantee either side, as they both know who they are dealing with when the contract is signed.

At present, this system of dealing is working well as a mechanism for moving large sums of money among a small number of investors. But, if the market is to expand, it will become necessary for the brokers to complete the deals they arrange.

In addition to the above-mentioned practices, there are two other forms of dealing to discuss in relation to the Kuwaiti market. One of these is the method of share-swaps, 'where a block of shares in one company is exchanged for shares in another at a valuation with no money changing hands'. (21) Such deals occur frequently and tend to be in large lines of stock. The other form is the system of forward dealing where two dealers agree on a forward deal at an agreed price, normally a premium on the current market price, the seller then delivers the shares where he receives a post-dated cheque for the amount due.

Attempts have been made by the authorities to regulate the system of forward dealing but to no avail, as these were not accepted by big traders. Other attempts to impose regulatory laws on the system of dealing were introduced in 1984 with the opening of the Kuwaiti stock exchange building by the Kuwait Securities Market Committee. One of the rules is that the market management specify the time and place of conducting transactions related to financial papers negotiable in the stock exchange. Another is the fact that a dealer is not allowed to choose for himself whom to deal with. To complement this, the brokers are put under the obligation of making a settlement if their clients fail to do so. Although this method does not meet the 'rule that the broker takes total responsibility for settlement vis-à-vis the market, which is the customary practice in every other world market, this is a novelty in Kuwait and a distinct advance on the previous practice'. (22) This was introduced to ensure that individual brokers combined their business into stronger units.

Still another regulation is the adoption in trading of the method of written bidding where 'the broker must write down the information related to the transaction he intends to conduct for the account of his customer on the board for the purpose'. (23) After completion of offers and bids, dealing arrangements should be carried on under the supervision of the market management. Article II stipulates that brokers are required, when regarding price or volume quotation, to keep any variation in price quotations within four units plus or minus the previous closing price, and not to exceed the fixed maximum volume of dealing of 25 units or go below the minimum of one unit.

The law also imposes on brokers the duty not to

manipulate prices, give false or misleading information, and conduct deals not involving any change of beneficial ownership. But despite these laws, the system is not sufficiently supervised to detect a breach of the law.

E **Problems**

Prior to the issue on 14 August 1984 of the decree regulating the securities market, the stock market faced problems which were the result of the negative practices in the market during the 1970s and early 1980s. One of the features was speculation, which was the result of the desire on the part of dealers to make quick profits, thus rendering share prices in the market inconsistent with their real value. In fact, the speculation which the local market witnessed contributes to the continuous inflationary trends in the domestic economy, and hinders the market's role in economic development.

Another problem was investors' rush to subscribe. In the 1970s and early 1980s the demand for company shares in the primary market could have been used by the securities market to mobilise and channel savings in the interest of the domestic economy. 'Nevertheless, this market phenomenon contributed to the creation of speculation in funders' shares, and the sale of eligibility to subscribe, which led to sharp rises in share prices.' (24) But still, this phenomenon succeeded in concentrating the shares in the hands of a few big investors who were then able to control the market activity.

Still another problem was the narrow domestic base for investment in Kuwait which has given rise to speculation in shares and real estate, because these constituted easy investment outlets giving spontaneous high profit within a short time.

The market also suffers from the similarities of active traders, who, because they share the same motivation, tend to push the market in the same direction. As a result, the market is either soaring upward on high volume or slumping down. In addition the market suffers from the absence of formal, centralised price-making mechanisms similar to those in other markets. Also, brokers do not guarantee completion of the deal as is normally practised elsewhere.

Following the Al-Manakh crisis, the stock exchange committee saw the opportunity to gain public acceptance for a more structured and disciplined market.

II   BAHRAIN STOCK MARKET

Following the collapse of the unofficial Kuwaiti stock market (Al-Manakh), the Bahraini authorities started to talk seriously of establishing a formal stock exchange. Previously, the sale of shares took place in a local market where confidence diminished because of several factors: concern about oil prices, the effect of the collapse of the unofficial Kuwaiti stock exchange, and the flight of capital caused by the war in Iran and Iraq. The impact of these factors resulted in share prices falling by 50 per cent in 1983. This fall in prices also affected those local companies that did not deal on the Manakh.

To prevent further deterioration, the Ministry decided not to follow the example of Kuwait, where the Government pumped in money to get the market moving again. The Minister of Commerce thought that once an official stock exchange was set up, natural market forces would bring about an improvement in the market. The Ministry's first step was to open an information centre in August 1983 after a study by the International Finance Corporation into the various types of stock exchange the country could adopt. This move was welcomed by local bankers because they saw it as a prelude to a full exchange which would help prevent speculation. Habib Kassem, the Commerce and Agriculture Minister, suggested that a Bahraini stock exchange could act as a regional centre for trading shares in companies based in other Gulf co-operation countries.

On the other hand, local sources preferred to see an exchange grow out of the existing brokerage system, which the country had regulated in May 1982. Under these regulations, the brokers must deposit financial guarantees with the Ministry of Commerce and Agriculture, which then issues them with a yearly licence. Under the information centre laws, brokers were able to keep a closer watch on day-to-day transactions. Through this monitoring system the 19 registered brokers were encouraged to notify the Ministry of transactions, which are then telexed to other brokers. This regulation acts as an 'interim measure designed to inform participants of what is going on in the market and to help formulate Stock Exchange Law'. (25)

The need for regulated investment and investment

advice had also produced companies set up specifically for that purpose. One such company is the Arabian Investment Banking Corporation established in 1982 to offer advice to shareholders and to encourage investors to invest locally. 'This Corporation hopes to advise some of the local trading and contracting companies on structuring their operations to achieve maximum profit, and this may involve sales or public quoting divisions within the companies.' (26) A law to define the operations of a full stock exchange is still being drafted, whereby planning will 'cover trading of 32 companies, 19 local public joint stock companies, and 13 exempt companies'. (27) Such a development will depend on a resolution of Kuwaiti debts resulting from the Al-Manakh collapse which would enable the companies to resume normal operations and 'improve liquidity for the more solid investment opportunities that a Bahraini stock exchange will offer'. (28)

The first formal stock exchange in Bahrain was established in 1984, although formal trading will not commence before the end of 1987. The exchange office is small, listing the shares of only 32 companies, 19 local companies and 13 exempt companies. The 19 registered brokers operate within the guidelines of the brokerage regulations introduced in 1982. Brokers are required to notify the Ministry of Commerce and Agriculture of all transactions. Also, listed companies are required to disclose, via the brokers, financial information that may be relevant to their share prices.

The new stock exchange is operating a two-tier trading system in order to protect the local market. Bahraini citizens are permitted to trade in shares of Bahraini companies, while non-residents and nationals are permitted to trade in shares of offshore companies, and companies that have listings on other foreign stock exchanges.

The Ministry of Commerce proposed controls to establish a finalised system of buying and selling shares and to ensure publication of closing prices and trading volumes. At present, the Ministry publishes a summary of daily transactions. Despite the fact that the banking sector had been in support of the new stock exchange, formal trading has not commenced yet, and the establishment of a Bahraini stock exchange still awaits the decision of the GCC countries.

III SAUDI ARABIA STOCK MARKET

Shaping the future of the Saudi stock market depends upon the agreement of the Ministers of Commerce and Finance on how the market should advance and be regulated. Saudi has housed a secondary shares market which is informal and unofficial, where stock in some 60 companies is traded and where trading is handled by about a dozen unlicensed brokers.

In January 1978 the deputy Commerce Minister announced that within two years there would be a regular stock exchange. However, the government, mindful of the crisis with the Souq-al-Manakh in Kuwait in 1982, issued in April 1983 a royal decree announcing that trading and registration of shares would be taken over by the country's domestic banks. This led to feelings of uncertainty in the market place and share prices fell back sharply. This was a change from the boom years of 1981 and 1982 when investors and speculators made money because shares hardly ever went down. Nevertheless, although business has fallen on hard times, the market is now gearing up for a public offering of shares in the state-owned Saudi Basic Industries Corporation (SABIC). Around 10 per cent to 15 per cent of SABIC shares are offered in the market with a total value estimated to be $430 million 'in line with the government's long standing commitment to privatise as much of state business as is practical'. (29) It is also estimated that by the end of 1990, over 50 per cent of SABIC stock will be in private hands and that several companies belonging to Petromin, the state oil company, will be privatised.

One reason for such a move is that there are a limited number of public companies with stocks to offer and so much private money looking for investment outlets. Such public companies number around 50, including banks, factories, the bus company, a shipping company, and a hotel chain as well as some agricultural companies, but with little turnover.

Until now, the Saudi market has been lacking in uniform stock quotations, company news and reporting requirements, although the government has provided some regulation in the form of decrees. The government also created a company for the registration of sales and chose the banks to broker and register shares on behalf of their customers. These moves will 'create a more homogeneous market and prices and also will allow the public to deal in stocks at about 450 bank branches'. (30) They will also enable the Saudi Arabia Monetary Agency (SAMA) to exert strict control over the market.

Already, some of the existing independent brokers who did not change their ways of dealing have been affected. Although few brokers have been recruited by the banks to work in the shares departments, or to trade shares on behalf of both private and corporate customers, other brokers are still dealing illegally. They claim that they 'took the initiative and the risk (to create a market) and provided an outlet for investors'. (31)

The recent regulations adopted by the government to protect the market against the adverse effects of speculation and to develop it gradually into a mature financial market have resulted in a significant progress of the capital market in Saudi Arabia.

At the end of 1984 the committee formulated executive rules regulating trading in shares through local banks, which entitled only licensed Saudi banks to conduct services related to the purchase and sale of the shares of Saudi joint-stock companies, and prohibited share trading by other than authorised banks.

The committee then delegated the supervision committee to supervise trading in shares, apply rules and regulations, develop regulations, obtain information on share transactions from commercial banks and companies, block dealing in the shares of a certain company, and halt all dealings in the market.

In addition, SAMA has established the shares control section assigned with the following tasks:

(1) determining office hours for dealing in shares at banks;
(2) determining the daily trading transactions coming to it from banks;
(3) supervising the appointment of employees at the trading units;
(4) registering and handling complaints of shareholders and adopting regulating measures;
(5) publishing share prices in local papers.

Banks had to allocate a separate trading unit at their head office to finalise trading transactions with other banks. A Saudi broker will be appointed to operate the unit. The broker's job is to ensure that all documents and data pertaining to a trading transaction are complete and correct.

Trading in shares should be confined to the shares of shareholding companies owned by Saudis, and to Saudi joint-stock companies. The customer is ordered to fill a purchase or sale order form indicating his name and the maximum amount which he wants to pay in case of purchase and the minimum amount in case of sale. The bank then charges a one per cent commission against finalising the operation.

NOTES

1.   El-Beblawi, H., and Fahmi, R. (1982) The Kuwaiti stock market 1946-1980, Kuwait: The Industrial Bank of Kuwait, p. 24.

2.   Ibid. p. 25.

3.   Kuwait Central Bank (1982) Economic Report, p. 72.

4.   Kuwait Stock Market Round Up (1980) The Middle East, 30 June.

5.   Kuwait Central Bank (1981) Economic Report, p. 91.

6.   Ibid. p. 92.

7.   Kuwait Central Bank (1980-1983) Economic Report, p. 92.

8.   Ibid. p. 92.

9.   Ibid. p. 93.

10.   Kuwait Central Bank (1983) Economic Report, p. 78.

11.   Kuwait Central Bank (1982) Economic Report, p. 77.

12.   Kuwait Central Bank (1980-1983) Economic Report, p. 92.

13.   Kuwait Central Bank (1982) Economic Report, p. 89.

14.   Ibid. p. 67.

15.   Kuwait Central Bank (1980) Economic Report. p. 76.

16.   Kuwait Central Bank (1981) Economic Report, p. 90.

17.   Kuwait Central Bank (1982) Economic Report, p. 70.

18.   'Kuwait securities market needs better organisation' (1981) The Arab Economist, vol. 13, December.

19.   Whelar, J. (ed.) (1985) 'Kuwait', Middle East

Economic Digest Practical Guide, p. 88.

20. Hollis, J. (1981) 'The Kuwait and other stock markets in the Arab world' in Field, P. and Moore, A., Arab financial markets, (eds) London: Euromoney Publications, p. 79.

21. Ibid. p. 79.

22. 'The new stock exchange' (1984) Mid East Markets, vol. 11, no. 22, 29 October.

23. Kuwait Central Bank (1980-1984), Economic Report, p. 99.

24. Ibid. p. 94.

25. Shirreff, D. (1984) 'No-one's trading Bahraini shares', Euromoney, May.

26. 'Stock exchange takes shape', Middle East Economic Digest: Special Report, September 1983, p. 47.

27. Ibid. p. 47.

28. Ibid.

29. 'Saudi Arabia: regulation; the stock market', Euromoney, November 1984.

30. Heller, B. (1983) 'Saudi Arabia keeps tight rein on flourishing stock market', Herald International Tribune, a Special Report, Part ii, 30 September.

31. Ibid.

Chapter Three

STOCK MARKETS IN THE LEVANT COUNTRIES

I THE AMMAN FINANCIAL MARKET

A Historical background (1976-1980)

The call for the establishment of a financial market in
Jordan was first brought to attention in the three-year
development plan (1973-75) and later in the five-year
development plan (1976-80). These plans, with their heavy
investments, necessitated the establishment of an
institution that would take up the mobilisation of these
investments. The hundreds of public shareholding companies
that existed in Jordan were able to mobilise large amounts
of domestic and foreign savings and financial contributions.
Also, the government put all its efforts into mobilising funds
to finance its development projects, especially the issue of
public debts. The development of a financial market in
Jordan required all these variables to be considered.

In June 1976, the authorities issued provisional law no.
31 of the Amman financial market, 'which provides a basic
framework for new issue regulation, disclosure, financial
reporting, supervision of the exchange, and monitoring of
insider trading and price manipulation'. (1) According to
article 50, the Minister of Finance has the power to fix the
date on which dealing in financial papers shall start on the
market floor. Article 3 defines the status of the Amman
financial market as having a legal personality and financial
autonomy and enjoying full legal capacity and the right to
appoint an attorney. The market shall also be considered a
public institution practising commercial transactions in
dealing with others and subject to the provisions of the

commerce law.

Article 4 prescribes the objectives of the market as follows:

(1) promote savings by activity and encouraging investments in financial papers, and to direct such savings for the development of the national economy;
(2) organise and control issues of, and dealings in, financial papers, so as to ensure the soundness, ease and speed of such dealings and to guarantee the financial interest of the country and the protection of small savers; and
(3) gather and publish the statistics and information necessary to realise the social objectives.

Article 2 defines the financial papers as the negotiable shares, bills and bonds issued in Jordan by the government, government institutions, or public and private Jordanian shareholding companies, or any other negotiable financial papers.

Article 6 stipulates that every Jordanian public shareholding company whose paid up capital totals JD 100,000 and above must be listed in the market. As for other shareholding companies, applying to list their shares does not depend on the size of their capital.

Despite all that has been said and done, the market did not start its operations as a public financial institution with its own legal status and financial independence until January 1978. The Amman financial market was set up as 'both a market for securities trading and a regulatory agency for the securities market'. (2) Its responsibility lies in the promotion and development of both the primary and secondary markets in Jordan, as well as in the organisation of the participants' activities in the market and their provision of the necessary expertise. Thus, in setting up a formal exchange, the government 'has brought the brokers together under one roof, established regular trading hours, and posted daily lists in the local newspapers giving the latest stock prices'. (3)

The management of the market is the responsibility of a board consisting of six members appointed by the Council of Ministers. These members represent the central bank, commercial banks and specialised credit institutions, representatives from listed companies and the controller of companies in the Ministry of Industry and Trade and the Amman Chamber of Industry. The chairman of the board also holds the office of general manager of the Amman financial market.

Trading of securities takes place on the floor through registered brokers licensed by the Amman financial market board. The brokers number nine, five of which were private shareholding companies with a total capital of JD 120,000 and four ordinary public companies with a total capital of JD 50,000. The number of brokers reached eleven by the end of 1978 with the inclusion of the Arab Finance Corporation (a public shareholding company with a capital of JD 2 million) and the Arab Jordan Investment Bank (a public shareholding company with a capital of JD 5 million). These two new institutions will concentrate their market activities on underwriting new securities issues as well as financial advisory services.

The Amman financial market showed considerable success during its first year of operation. This could be seen from the volume of transactions in shares, in publishing the prices at which transactions were made and also in publishing financial information which is of concern to company shareholders.

Although relatively small compared with trading on other markets, the volume of the exchange has been very successful, as its chairman and general manager, Dr Sabbagh, had forecast that it would be.

During 1978, the public shareholding companies listed on the market numbered 66, 'with 83.5 million shares having a market value of over JD 200 million'. (4) However, only 57 companies traded their shares on the market where 'the total value of transactions reached JD 5.6 million, which represents about 2.4 million shares'. (5)

As far as the value of trading is concerned, industrial shares came in first place with 0.88 million at a market value of JD 2.89 million, thus representing 51.4 per cent of the total volume traded in 1978. The banking sector came in second place, where 1.01 million shares of ten banks were traded at a market value of JD 1.91 million accounting for 34 per cent of total volume. The service sector followed with 0.4 shares traded at a market value of JD 0.61 million or 10.8 per cent of total volume. Finally, came the insurance sector where eleven companies traded 0.08 million shares at a market value of JD 0.21 million. (See Table 3.1).

In part, this increase in volume is accounted to the listing and trading of the government's ten-year development bonds which previously had been either held

Table 3.1: Activities of the Amman financial market 1978

Sectors	Number of traded shares (in millions)	Volume of trading (in millions)	Number of companies
Industry	0.88	2.89	26
Banking	1.01	1.91	10
Services	0.46	0.61	10
Insurance	0.08	0.21	11
Totals	2.43	5.62	57

Source: Central Bank of Jordan, Fifteenth Annual Report, 1978.

until maturity or sold back to the central bank at par value because of the absence of a secondary market. This move, according to an economist at the central bank, was taken to 'attract investments from rich neighbouring countries which have few outlets for investment inside their own borders'. (6) Another move by the stock exchange authorities was to amend the laws to enable non-Jordanian Arab citizens to invest freely in Jordanian companies through the exchange. In the past, foreigners were required to obtain permission from the Council of Ministers before buying or selling shares of a Jordanian company. 'Now the Amman financial market handles such matters directly and Jordan's laws remain liberal in regard to repatriation of dividends or proceeds from a sale.' (7) Such a move is seen by the authorities as a stimulant to trading in the exchange market.

The year 1979 saw further expansion in the trading activities of the Amman financial market to include negotiable certificates of deposit, Jordan government development bonds, when 'eleven bond issues are listed on the stock exchange floor, with a total outstanding market value of some JD 60 million', (8) and bonds issued by shareholding companies. Private corporate bonds begin to float when 'a royal decree has been issued providing them with the same tax exemptions on interest earned as the state's development bonds'. (9) Also, Citibank issued JD denominated certificates of deposit that carry maturities of one, three, six and twelve months to be listed and traded on the stock exchange. Thus, the addition of government and corporate bond trading in 1979 resulted in a huge increase in the total volume and value of exchange. Total value in 1979 showed an increase of 182 per cent over 1978 (JD 15.845 million in 1979 compared with JD 5.62 million in 1978) with the value of shares traded reaching 6.53 million. Trading in shares of banks and other financial institutions came first, representing JD 6.84 million of the 1979 total value, and 3.03 million of the volume. Industrial shares came second, with JD 6.7 million and volume of 2.00 million, 'while shares traded in the service sector companies were worth JD 1.31 million and volume of 1.29 million and JD 0.93 or 0.21 million shares for insurance companies'.(10) According to Dr Sabbagh, the market manager, the reason for the 'increase in business has been the entry of institutional investors into the securities market place'. (11) Also, around 10 per cent of trading consisted of shares purchased by Jordanians working in the Gulf. Moreover, 1979 saw an increase in the number of Jordanian companies trading their shares in the market. (See Table 3.2).

Table 3.2: Activities of the Amman financial market in 1979

Sectors	Number of traded shares (in millions)	Volume of trading (in millions)	Number of companies
Industry	2.00	6.76	32
Banking	3.03	6.84	13
Services	1.29	1.31	11
Insurance	0.21	0.93	14
Totals	6.53	15.84	70

Source: Central Bank of Jordan, Sixteenth Annual Report, 1979.

B Development (1980-1984)

The 1980s witnessed the further expansion of the Amman stock exchange to include the active participation of merchant banking-type institutions; the extension of tax-free status to bonds issued on behalf of private borrowers and those listed with central bank bonds on the market; the refinancing by Jordanian banks of international credits for local borrowers; and most important of all, the issuing of the first local negotiable certificates of deposit; the social security fund and the pension fund when transformed into investment companies 'promise to become a major domestic financing force in the coming years'. (12) The pension fund's change of status into that of an investment company will enable the government to 'run the pension paying scheme that the pension fund in any case cannot fully finance from its own resources', (13) and will lead the government also to concentrate on investing the fund's current assets of some JD 22 million in local industrial projects. In addition, the social security corporation will prod local investment financing through accumulating obligatory payments from workers and employers.

In a bid to attract regional capital, and to expand its role in promoting institutional links between Jordanian, Arab and European securities houses and investment banks, the central bank established the Jordanian securities company to provide more sophisticated services in the securities field. According to its manager, one of the priorities of the company will be its activity 'as financial intermediary between the local market and the regional and international markets, particularly by expanding links with brokerage houses in other countries'. (14) This came at a time of more flourishing activities in the local market, such as the move by some public institutions in the Gulf to buy Jordanian shares, the large amount of money flowing into Jordan due to the reliance of the national budget on foreign budget support, the high level of remittances from Jordanians working abroad, and rising income from tourism. All this encouraged investors as well as ordinary savers to look for new means of investing their cash.

The rapid growth of business on the Amman financial market urged its directors to introduce the use of computers. Whereas before, transactions were dealt with manually - thus creating a huge paper workload for the staff - the installation of this new system will enable them to deal with the rising business more efficiently. At the moment, deals are restricted to Jordan itself, but it is hoped that the stock exchange could be linked with others such as the London, New York and Tokyo stock exchanges, to step up international trading.

Still a further development was the abolition of an additional fee which had been levied on all transactions since February 1982, in order to activate the secondary market. The lowering of fees was met with approval by the investors. Around the same time that the extra transactions fees were introduced, a parallel market was set up 'as a tool for absorbing extra liquidity in the stock exchange, and to implement the Amman financial markets policy of guaranteeing investors' safety by more disclosure about securities'. (15)

In this over-the-counter market, brokers will trade stock of newly established companies in a separate session at the stock exchange premises. The new market is for shares in firms which cannot be listed on the Amman financial market or which have their dealings reported outside the market until they have issued an annual report with financial statements covering their first year of operations. Only public shareholding companies with at least half their capital paid up are admitted to this new market. According to the market director, Dr Sabbagh, about 20 firms were represented on the first day of trading, and he expected the number to increase to at least 30 by the end of 1982. Firms on the over-the-counter market are not listed with the stock exchange and dealings will not be reported daily in the press. Late 1982 also saw the beginning of the recession which prevailed in Jordan until 1984. The factors which played a major role in this recession are both external and internal.

External factors include:

(1) The continuation of international economic recession, the unstable condition of the international money market and the down trend in economic growth rates of the world economy.
(2) The international recession lowered the industrial countries consumption of energy and as a result the decrease in oil exports, oil prices, and the revenues of the Arab oil producing countries. Some of the Arab Gulf states were faced with tight economic problems portrayed in major cuts in their budgets.
(3) The unstable political situation which has affected the region.
(4) The decline in financial assistance to Jordan because of the unfulfilled commitments of financial aid by Arab countries.
(5) The Arab Gulf States' inability to continue importing Jordanian products, investing in Jordan, or having Jordanian employees as before. Jordan is dependent to a large degree on the Gulf markets.

(6) The Kuwaiti owned Jordanian shares were liquidised to meet their financial obligation to creditors due to the collapse of the Al Manakh market and the resulting financial crisis in Kuwait.

Internal factors include:

(1) All sectors of the Jordanian economy were affected by the international economic recession.
(2) The decline of the growth ratios of some local economic indicators and the slow-down of economic growth.
(3) The decrease of Arab assistance to Jordan resulted in a shortage of available financial resources. This accounts for the cuts in government spending, and in the implementation of some Jordanian planned projects being postponed.
(4) The decrease in volume of Jordanian exports by 14 per cent due to the prevailing market situation in neighbouring Arab states. This has been reflected in the financial results of Jordanian industrial companies and tight financial positions in some financial institutions.
(5) The shortage of floating liquidity resulted in a decrease in the prices of companies' shares.
(6) The noticeable increase in the number of publicly-held companies licensed to perform the same objectives in the service sector. Some of these companies deviated from their objectives because the feasibility studies of these companies were prepared without any scientific analysis of objectives and the ways of attaining them, and the need of the Jordanian market for their services.
(7) Some of the companies founded in the 1970s did not show any improvement in their operations.
(8) The decision of the Ministry of Industry and Commerce to increase the capital of insurance companies affected the price of shares in these companies. It also affected the process of covering the offered shares for public subscription in the primary market.
(9) The central bank's decisions to increase the capital base of some commercial banks, and the long implementation period given to these banks, played a major role in liquidating many shares, because investors wanted to keep their cash on standby for the new public offering for subscription by those banks.
(10) The expectation by the Jordanian investors of the low

profit generated by the majority of listed companies affected the prices of most shares of listed companies.

(11) The decrease in the number of tourists visiting Jordan affected operations of companies serving the tourism sector.

C   Activities 1980-1986

During 1980, the number of shares traded tripled compared with 1979. Despite the decline in the number of listed corporations by four to 66, the volume of shares traded increased by 174.1 per cent to reach 17.3 million shares, while the total market value of traded shares was JD 41.3 million, an increase of 161.6 per cent. When we break down the stocks traded by sector we see that the number of stocks traded in the financial sector reached 7.6 million shares with a value amounting to JD 17.34 million or 42 per cent of the total value. The industrial sector came second in terms of shares traded with a total of 5.1 million shares with a value of JD 17.22 million or 28 per cent; services 4.4 million with a value of JD 6 million or 25 per cent and the insurance sector was last with 0.2 million shares with a value of JD 0.93 million or 1 per cent of the total.

In 1981, the Amman financial market achieved great progress compared with previous years. The figures doubled to reach 29.23 million traded shares while the total value reached JD 75.42 million. The breakdown of shares traded by sector shows that the number of shares traded in industry increased to 13.90 million with a value of JD 32.07 million or 47.5 per cent of total number of traded shares, the banking sector came second with 9.83 million shares traded and total value of JD 28.90 million followed by the services and insurance sectors with traded shares of 4.63 million and 0.87 million and total value of JD 7.83 and JD 6.62 millions respectively.

What was noticeable during 1981 was that dealings were centred around shares with nominal values. For the one-dinar shares, the volume traded increased to 27.3 million, a 97.1 per cent of total increase of traded shares. Thus, their value went up to JD 50.6 million or 69.1 per cent of the total increase in the market value of traded shares. On the other hand, the value of shares traded with nominal value of JD 10.0 went up by JD 7.3 million and those of two dinars by JD 0.5 million. 'This trend reflected a wider participation of small savers and investors in the Amman financial market transactions which, in turn, help by mobilising national savings and investing them in various economic sectors.' (16)

1982 saw the listing on the market of 86 companies, of which only 82 traded their shares on the market. Trading in shares 'went up by 18.4 per cent to reach 34.6 million shares, compared with a rise of 63.3 per cent in 1981. The total market value of traded shares in 1982 was JD 112.25 million, an increase of 48.8 per cent compared with 82 per cent in the previous year.' (17) Also, the service sector showed an increase in its traded shares of 7.10 million shares or 46 per cent of total increase, whereas the relative importance of the service sector rose to 20.5 per cent, the industrial and banking shares decreased to 42.5 per cent and 31.7 per cent respectively. By contrast, the banking sector showed an increase in the volume of trading to reach 10.97 million and the market value of traded shares went up by JD 49.09 or 69.9 per cent, followed by the service sector which went up by JD 14.52 million or 85.4 per cent with the volume of traded shares at 7.10 million. The volume of trading in insurance and industrial shares went up by 33.1 per cent and 24.2 per cent - by 1.83 million and 14.70 million and JD 8.81 million and JD 39.83 million respectively.

Dealings on shares with small nominal values continued to rise. The traded volume of one-dinar shares increased to 32.84 million in 1982 and the traded value of shares went up to JD 83.42 million. On the other hand, the traded volume of other shares reflected a slight decrease.

Because of the economic recession that hit the Amman financial market, the number of shares traded in 1983 reached 36.2 million with a market value of JD 119.4 million. This downward trend, which involved the prices of most shares traded, was attributed to a number of factors which I have previously listed. The shares of banks increased to 16.4 million traded during 1983, while the number of shares of sectors such as industry, service and insurance became 13.3 million, 5.1 million and 1.4 million respectively.

Also, the market value of banks' traded shares rose by JD 86.9 million or 77.1 per cent, while those of industry and mining, services and insurance sectors, dropped by 47.7 per cent, 54.5 per cent and 42.0 per cent respectively. The increase of trading in bank shares 'was partly due to the easy disposal of them when the need for liquidity arises and to the relatively higher return on them'. (18) The continuation of the economic recession which hit Jordan in 1982 is still felt in the number of shares traded which reached 28.2 million with a total market value of JD 52.9 million in 1984. The decline in activity hit all sectors but was most noticeable in the banks and finance companies whose shares traded dropped to 10.7 million shares with a market value of JD 33 million. The industrial companies followed where shares dropped by 12.4 million shares with a total market value of JD 14.6 million. The services sector came third with the number of shares traded at 3.2 million and a total market value of JD 2.8 million. Only shares of insurance companies increased by 1.9 million but their market value sank to JD 2.5 million.

During 1985 the Amman financial market showed considerable improvement despite the economic slowdown which had begun in 1982. The number of shares traded reached 31.25 million with a total market value of JD 64.32 million. This improvement was most noticeable in the banking sector whose shares had risen from 10.7 million in 1984 to 15.72 million in 1985, with a total market value of JD 47.09 million against JD 33 million in 1984. On the other hand, the industrial sector was hit, when shares dropped from 12.4 million shares with a total market value of JD 14.6 million in 1984 to 9.93 million shares with a total market value of JD 11.85 million in 1985. Trading in the shares of services and insurance companies had also shown a slight decline, where the shares had dropped from 3.19 million to 4.22 million and 1.95 million to 1.38 million, with a total market value of JD 2.81 and 2.57 millions respectively.

This improvement of trading in the banking sector shares may be attributed to two factors. The first is the relatively high return on these shares; the second is due to the issuing of new shares by several commercial banks after the decision of the central bank to raise the capital of each commercial bank to a minimum of JD 5.0. The decline in trading in industrial shares is attributed to 'the continuation of economic recession and the adverse effect it has had on the prices of shares and on their yields'. (19)

The improvement which the Amman financial market had shown in 1985 continued into 1986. The number of shares traded reached 39.9 million with a total market value of JD 64.8 million in 1986 compared with 31.25 million

Table 3.3: Activities of the Amman financial market: value of trading in 1980-1986 (millions JDs)

Sector	1980	1981	%	1982	%	1983	%
Banking	17.34	28.90	66.7	49.09	69.9	86.9	77.4
Industrial	17.22	32.07	86.2	39.83	24.2	20.8	-47.7
Service	6.00	7.83	31.8	14.52	85.4	6.6	-54.5
Insurance	0.93	6.62	611.8	8.81	33.1	5.1	-42.0
Total	41.43	75.42	82.0	112.25	48.8	119.4	6.4

Sector	1983	1984	%	1985	%	1986	%
Banking	86.9	33.0	-62.0	47.1	42.7	39.1	-16.9
Industrial	20.8	14.6	-30.0	11.8	-19.2	18.3	55.1
Service	6.6	2.8	-57.5	2.8	0	3.1	10.7
Insurance	5.1	2.5	-51.0	2.5	0	4.2	6.8
Total	119.4	52.9	-55.7	64.2	21.4	64.7	0.8

Source: Amman Financial Market, Statistical Bulletin, 1978-1986

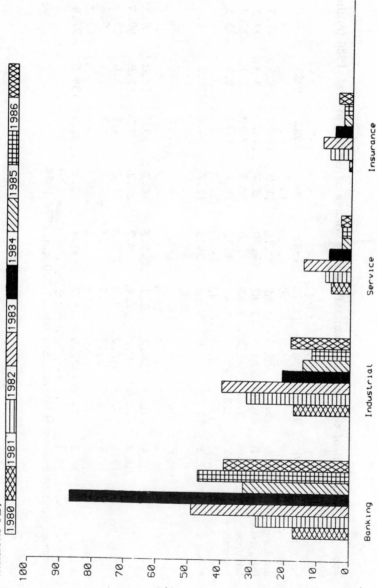

Figure 3.1: Activities of the Amman financial market: value of trading in 1980-1986 (in millions JD)

Table 3.4: Activities of the Amman financial market: volume of trading in 1980-1986 (million shares)

Sector	1980	1981	%	1982	%	1983	%
Banking	7.6	9.83	29.3	10.97	11.9	16.4	49.5
Industrial	5.1	13.90	172.5	14.70	5.7	13.3	-9.5
Service	4.4	4.63	-5.2	7.10	53.5	5.1	-28.0
Insurance	.2	.87	335.0	1.83	128.7	1.4	-23.5
Total	17.3	29.23	68.9	34.6	18.7	36.2	1.6

	1983	1984	%	1985	%	1986	%
Banking	16.4	10.7	-34.7	15.7	46.7	17.0	8.3
Industrial	13.3	12.4	-6.8	9.9	-20.2	15.9	60.6
Service	5.1	3.2	-37.2	4.2	31.2	5.0	19.0
Insurance	1.4	1.9	35.7	1.3	-31.8	1.9	0.6
Total	36.2	28.2	-22.0	31.1	10.3	39.8	27.9

Source: Amman Financial Market, Statistical Bulletin, 1978-1986

Figure 3.2: Activities of the Amman financial market: volume of trading in 1980-1986

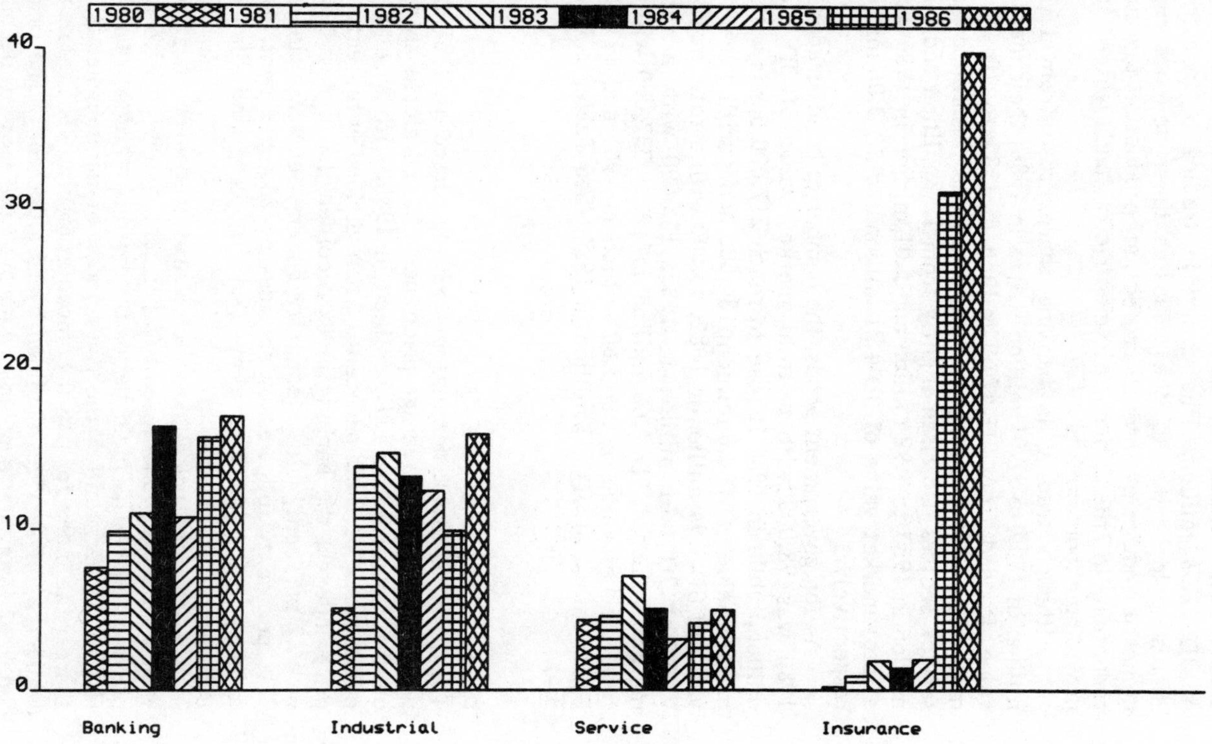

Legend: 1980 1981 1982 1983 1984 1985 1986

Categories: Banking, Industrial, Service, Insurance

shares and JD 64.32 million in 1985. The improvement in 1986 was not apparent in industrial stocks where around 15.99 million shares were traded with a total market value of JD 18.34 million. This upturn in trading in industrial shares could be due to 'the measures taken to encourage domestic industries through protection, production tax cuts reduction in the prices of electricity and water and providing export outlets'. (20)

Although trading in banking shares rose from 15.72 million in 1985 to 17.01 million shares in 1986, their market value dropped from JD 47.09 million in 1985 to JD 39.16 million in 1986. Trading in the shares of insurance and service sectors had risen slightly from 1.38 million and 4.22 million in 1985 to 1.92 million and 5.01 million in 1986 with a total market value of JD 4.21 million and JD 3.06 million respectively.

As for government bonds, the number of bonds traded in 1980 was 98,000 with a total market value of JD 1.66 million, while in 1981 it rose to reach 217,000 bonds with a market value of JD 2.3 million; 184,000 bonds with a market value of JD 1.94 million in 1982; 43,000 with a total market value of JD 0.61 million in 1983; 128,000 with a total market value of JD 1.68 million in 1984; 337,000 with a total market value of JD 3.60 million in 1985 and 121,000 bonds valued at JD 2.5 million in 1986. (See Tables 3.3 and 3.4).

Prices

The level of stock dealings in 1980 surpassed that of the previous year. The average price index for all stocks traded on the floor rose to 111.5 million in 1980, with a relative climb index of 33.2 per cent. When divided into sectoral price indexes, the banking index recorded the highest jump of 56.2 per cent, with electricity coming second, rising by 37.2 per cent, followed by services of 26.4 per cent. The industry price index rose by 18.1 per cent and that of insurance by 12.4 per cent.

In 1981 the price index for shares traded on the floor was 176.9 with an increase of 63 per cent compared with the previous year. The main factor behind this increase was the rise of 57 per cent in the price index of commercial bank shares; the index for power companies rose by 28.7 per cent, while that of services declined by 35.3 per cent. The price index of insurance companies improved the most to become

131.7 per cent.

In 1982 the average price index for shares traded on the floor rose to 203.5 and increased by 15.9 per cent. This was because of the increase in the price index of insurance companies and banks' shares, which went up by 11.6 per cent and 33.6 per cent respectively. Service company shares rose by 21.8 per cent. By contrast, those of power companies went down by 3.5 per cent.

In 1983 the developments that took place in the number of shares traded were reflected on the share price index. As shown by the central bank publication of share price indices, the index weighted by subscribed capital showed share prices to have dropped by 24.2 per cent to 153.4 points in 1983. Sector-wise, the biggest drop was in the shares of services and insurance companies - 32.7 per cent and 27.6 per cent respectively. According to the index weighted by the number of shares traded, the drop was much greater as the untraded shares prices were not considered. This index fell to 198.7 points in 1983, that is, by 24.6 per cent. Again, the fall was at its biggest level in the shares of services and insurance companies which fell by 42.6 per cent and 40.3 per cent respectively.

Economic conditions in 1984 caused further drops in share prices. The index of these prices weighted by subscribed capital dropped to 119.5 points, that is, by 33.3 per cent. Again, the drop was most pronounced in the prices of shares of services and insurance companies which fell by 21 per cent and 21 per cent, respectively. As for shares price index weighted by the number of shares traded, it went down by 30.1 per cent to 137.3 points. Again, the drop was sharpest in the case of insurance companies at 63.6 per cent, followed by service companies at 33.9 per cent and banks at 27.7 per cent. (See Table 3.5).

Although there was a slight improvement in share trading during 1985 compared with 1984, the improvement was not great. The index of share prices weighted by subscribed capital dropped to 127.0 points in 1985. The drop was noticeable in the case of services and insurance companies whose share price declined by 25.3 per cent and 13.1 per cent respectively. The drop for shares in industry was 5.7 per cent and 2.7 per cent for banks and finance companies. The traded shares price index as weighted by the number of shares traded showed a drop to 110.1 points in 1985. Share prices of services companies decreased by 17.6 per cent, banks 16.2 per cent and industrial companies 13.4

Table 3.5: Amman financial market: share price index in 1980–1986 (January 1980 = 100)

Sector	1980	1981	%	1982	%	1983	%
Banking	128.0	201.0	57.0	268.6	33.6	243.0	-9.5
Industrial	114.4	147.3	28.7	142.2	-3.5	103.9	-27.0
Service	103.4	140.0	35.3	170.5	21.8	114.7	-32.7
Insurance	102.0	236.4	131.7	263.8	11.6	190.9	-27.6
General Index	111.5	176.9	63.0	203.5	15.9	153.4	-24.2

	1983	%	1984	%	1985	%	1986	%
Banking	243.0		164.6	-78.4	112.0	-31.9	106.1	-5.3
Industrial	103.9		90.4	-13.0	85.0	-5.9	86.6	1.9
Service	114.7		90.7	-21.0	70.9	-21.8	59.1	-16.6
Insurance	190.9		151.0	-21.0	138.3	-8.4	146.7	6.1
Total	153.4		119.5	-33.3	110.1	-7.9	107.3	-2.5

Source: Amman Financial Market, Statistical Bulletin, 1978–1986

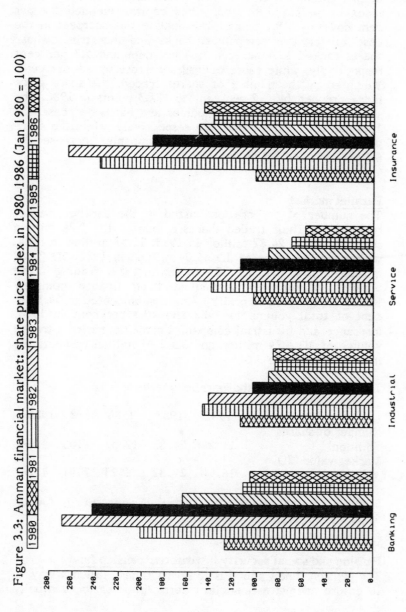

Figure 3.3: Amman financial market: share price index in 1980-1986 (Jan 1980 = 100)

per cent, while those of insurance companies increased by 45.1 per cent.

In 1986, share prices still had a downwards trend, despite the improvement in AFM activities. The share price index as weighted by subscribed capital declined 5.7 per cent down to 119.7 points. The decline was sharpest in the case of services companies, banks and industries, whose shares ranked 13.4 per cent, 64 per cent and 5.3 per cent respectively, while those of insurance rose by 9.4 per cent. Weighted by the number of shares traded, the share price index dropped by 2.5 per cent to 107.3 points in 1986. The share prices of services companies and banks decreased by 16.6 per cent and 5.3 per cent respectively, while the share prices of insurance and industrial companies increased by 6.1 per cent and 1.9 respectively.

Parallel market

The number of corporations listed in the parallel market reached 14. Their traded shares amounted to 11.24 million shares in 1982, 24.82 million in 1983, 12.57 million in 1984, with a market value of JD 16.04 million in 1982, JD 21.82 million in 1983 and JD 6.23 million in 1984. Trading in the parallel market was concentrated on finance company shares, whose volume of JD 8.7 million amounted to 54.3 per cent of total volume in 1982 and 40.3 per cent in 1983. Insurance and industrial companies came next with a traded volume of JD 4.74 million and JD 2.15 million respectively in 1982. (See Table 3.6).

Table 3.6: Trading in the 'parallel' market

	1982	1983	1984	1985	1986
Number of shares (million)	11.24	24.82	12.57	6.05	8.96
Market value (JD million)	16.04	21.82	6.23	2.41	4.76

Source: Central Bank of Jordan, Twenty-third Annual Report 1986, p. 27.

Pension and social security institutions' pension fund

The pension fund's policy is to invest funds in such a way as to ensure adequate financial returns 'in order to eventually shoulder the mounting financial burden of government pension obligations. To this end, the fund's investments continued to favour equity acquisition and/or participation, especially stocks of industrial enterprises.' (21)

The fund's total assets increased from JD 29.32 million in 1980 to 47.3 million in 1981, JD 54.78 million in 1982, JD 59.42 million in 1983, JD 58.48 million in 1984, JD 57.05 million in 1985 and 55.2 million in 1986, which represents an increase of 30.7 per cent, 15.9 per cent and 8.5 per cent respectively, with a drop of 1.6 per cent in 1984, 2.4 per cent in 1985 and 3.3 per cent in 1986. In order to maximise return on its financial resources, the fund increased its investments in stocks from JD 32.2 million in 1980 to JD 42.4 million in 1981, to JD 44.76 million in 1982, JD 48.46 million in 1983, and JD 48.44 million in 1984, while these dropped to JD 44.85 million in 1985 and JD 42.79 million in 1986. The relative importance of such investments in the total assets of the fund rose from 69.8 per cent in 1980 to 89.7 per cent in 1981, to 81.7 per cent in 1982, 81.6 per cent in 1983, 82.8 per cent in 1984, dropped to 78.6 per cent in 1985 and rose again to 81.1 per cent in 1986. On the other hand, the fund's holdings of bonds, whether government or corporate, decreased from JD 4.0 million in 1980, to JD 1 million in 1981, and remained steady at JD 1 million for 1982, 1983, 1984, 1985 and 1986. The fund's cash balances on hand and deposit at banks decreased from JD 3.7 million in 1980 to JD 2.2 million in 1981. These cash balances then fluctuated over the next five years as follows: JD 6.69 million in 1982, JD 7.42 in 1983, JD 6.17 million in 1984, JD 8.35m in 1985 and JD 7.92 million in 1986.

When we break down the fund's portfolio of corporate stock we notice that most of its investments in stocks are in industrial companies which amounted to JD 10.91 million in 1980 JD 30.7 million in 1981, JD 34.47 million in 1982, JD 68.6 million in 1983, JD 64.6 million in 1984, JD 67.6 million in 1985 and JD 60.7 million in 1986. This reflects the fund's development orientation.

Social security corporation

According to Social Security Law no. 30, whose aim is to provide the worker and his family with a permanent monthly income, the Social Security Corporation (SSC) was set up. The Corporation deducts from the monthly salary of those not covered by the Pension Law and invests the proceeds to meet most of its obligations towards those insured.

The SSC started its operations in 1980 by implementing its insurance against work injuries, occupational diseases, disability, old age and death. It then extended its coverage to include collecting deductions from all establishments employing 50 workers or more, and was further extended by the end of 1981 to private enterprises employing 20 workers or more.

In 1980, the total assets of the SSC amounted to JD 4.7 million, JD 17.2 million in 1981, JD 41.97 million in 1982, JD 66.52 million in 1983, JD 102.39 million in 1984, JD 135.68 million in 1985 and 179.8 million in 1986, which represented an increase of 26.7 per cent, 143.9 per cent, 58.5 per cent, 53.9 per cent, 32.5 per cent and 33.5 per cent respectively. The resources of the SSC have been used 'in line with its objectives and in areas of high profitability while maintaining enough liquidity to meet its current obligations'. (22) Most of the SSC's assets are deposits at banks as bonds and stocks. Those deposits amounted to JD 8.29 million in 1981, 22.46 million in 1982, JD 33.22 million in 1983, JD 35.64 million in 1984, JD 41.68 million in 1985 and JD 50.6 million in 1986, while its portfolio of stocks and bonds amounted to JD 5.66 million in 1981, JD 10.05 million in 1982, JD 17.99 million in 1983, JD 25.12 million in 1984, JD 56.10 million in 1985 and JD 57.7 million in 1986. 'While the SSC takes into consideration the well-known investment concerns of security, profitability and liquidity, it also considers national development priorities.' (23) As such, its investments total JD 6.74 million in projects in the following sectors: industry 75 per cent, finance companies and banks 8 per cent and services 17 per cent.

D Methods of dealing

The Amman financial market moved to a new building in 1982 and is in the process of being computerised. The market is open for trading every day except Friday. The auction method is used for trading, where the best bid and offer prices are noted by the brokers for each stock. Jobbers or specialists are not present in the market.

Transactions are carried out on a cash basis, but margin loans have been introduced by some brokers. Although the central bank is authorised to prohibit lending against securities, indirect lending to finance trading in securities takes place.

Although settlement usually takes place on the day of the transaction, delays of several weeks or even months in delivering the share certificates are possible. In the meantime, trading can continue to take place on the basis of temporary share certificates, despite its being problematic.

E **Problems**

(1) Trading which takes place on the basis of temporary share certificates is a dangerous practice which has led to problems in several other emerging markets. This means that there are delays in delivering actual shares and certificates.

(2) Lack of accurate flow of information from companies and Amman financial market operations on the yield of shares, to enable both existing and potential shareholders to assess performance accurately. One by-product would be that speculation and loss would stop if everyone was better informed.

(3) Some public shareholding companies were established without taking into account the needs of the economy. On the contrary, a large number of these established companies were of similar aims and competitiveness. For example, at some time there was a tendency to channel investment in the service sector instead of coming up with feasible projects in the manufacturing and agriculture sectors which the country needs to accelerate development.

(4) Problems of operation and management of insurance and financial corporation because of the security of personnel in these fields.

(5) The lack of development plans which could provide investors with helpful information on development priorities in general and new projects to be implemented by the public sector.

(6) The difficult economic environment and the prolonged and deepening recession in the world with the unstable money market conditions have resulted in the decline of revenues of Arab oil-producing countries. Thus, Jordan's economic growth, with its many sectors, was affected due to the decline in the financial assistance from these countries.

(7) Annual companies' reports: the economic recession showed that companies files were not edited properly

and did not follow accountancy rules - wrong figures were sometimes included in financial reports. This was because of the absence of people responsible for looking over the public shareholding companies.

(8) The lack of a clear role in the money market for the financial institutions. These institutions did not finance any investment in the secondary market, and did not go into the market as a buyer and seller which weakened their role as a market creator.

Despite all these problems, the financial market in Jordan has proved its viability and operated smoothly. But the challenge of this market still remains to be met, namely how to turn financial into real investment.

II BEIRUT STOCK MARKET

The Lebanese Stock Exchange was set up in August 1920, under a French mandate, by a group of French-Lebanese businessmen. In its early years, the exchange, known as the bourse, was only active in dealing in gold and foreign exchange with little stock activity. This was because of the limited number of companies listed on the bourse and because most were French companies which preferred to work on the Paris bourse. In those early days the Beirut bourse experienced a low daily volume of transactions. It was not until the mid-1950s that its activities increased, when the total volume of shares traded exceeded a million and a half Lebanese pounds annually.

Since 1964, however, the market has witnessed a declining volume to the extent that during some days no shares were traded at all, 'due to United States investment companies carrying out transactions outside the exchange market'. (24) The flourishing volume of business that lasted until 1964 was due to the increase in the listing of real estate corporations.

However, the downward trend that lasted until 1969 began with the failure of two banks that were heavily involved in real estate. This trend was made more acute by the feeling of uncertainty created by the 1966 Intra crisis, the central bank's strict control over commercial banks' portfolio investment, and the outflow of funds to earn higher interest in Euro dollar and United States markets. As a result, the total volume of trading in 1969 reached LL 2 million, only 3 per cent of the 1964 volume.

By the end of 1969, the companies listed on the exchange numbered 42, of which five were banks, ten real estate firms, two insurance companies, six electric power, 19 industrial firms, a concrete company, and two Treasury bills issues. Around one half of these companies did not have a market price and few were actively trading.

The stagnation of the Beirut exchange was attributed to an important factor; the increasing number of American and European brokerage firms. Although these firms succeeded in attracting a large volume of business, by the end of 1968 this ceased due to the continuing decline of the international stock markets during 1969 and early 1970. As such, many speculators and investors experienced a huge capital loss, and in turn re-channelled their funds into other forms of investment. As a result, a large number of these brokerage firms had to close.

Attempts by the government to bring life to the Beirut bourse were met with a lack of success. So, the bourse's activities remained limited and restricted to the speculation of wealthy individuals. It failed to stimulate greater investor interest and confidence and to act as a medium which savings could be channelled to long-term productive investment.

The beginning of 1971 saw a period of good activity on the stock exchange, and a regaining of confidence in stock investment due to the 'abundance of liquidities and the low money interest rate associated with the good rates of return on stocks'. (25) This feeling of prosperity resulted in an increase in the number of transactions between 1970 and 1974. With respect to the number of stocks negotiated, there was an increase of 101,240 in 1970, 126, 522 in 1971, 387,034 in 1972, 194,427 in 1973 and 385,267 in 1974. As for their monetary value, there was an increase of LL 10.4 million in 1970, LL 14.2 million in 1971, LL 42.4 million in 1972, LL 30.1 million in 1973 and LL 29.1 million in 1974.

But this general feeling of prosperity did not last long. The flaring up of the Lebanese civil war at the end of 1974 paralysed all economic activities and forced the stock exchange to close. The exchange did not resume its activities until 1977 due to damage to the exchange premises added to the problems arising from the loss of bearer stocks. These events, as a result, have created a very tricky situation as to the negotiation and transmission of stocks.

Table 3.7: Activities of the Beirut stock exchange: value and volume of traded shares in 1964-1983

	1964	1965	1966	1967	1968	1969	1970	1971	1972	1973	1974
No of stock transacted in millions	857	368	191	152	41	26	101	127	387	194	285
Monetary value of stock transacted in million LL	81	29	14	8	5	2	10	14	42	30	49

	1975	1976	1977	1978	1979	1980	1981	1982	1983
No of stock transacted in millions	closed	closed	43	closed	90	18	7	34	27
Monetary value of stock transacted in million LL	closed	closed	7	closed	25	2	.624	2	2

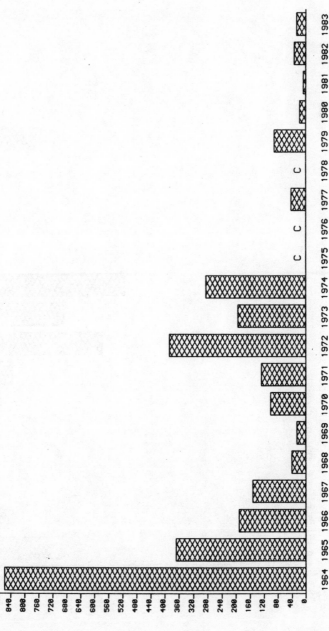

Figure 3.4: Activities of Beiruit stock exchange: number of stock transacted in 1964-1983 (in millions) ('C' means closed)

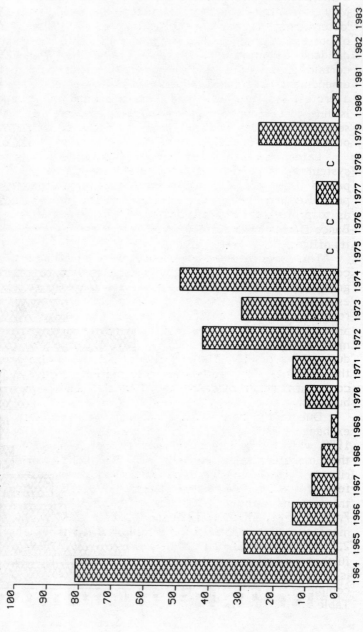

Figure 3.5: Activities of Beirut stock exchange: monetary value of stock transacted in 1964–1983 (in million LL) ('C' means closed)

In order to safeguard the rights of shareholders and restore confidence in investments, the stock exchange authorities prepared a draft law to regulate the situation. In May 1977 the Council of Ministers approved decree 41 'determining the procedure to be followed in all cases of loss of possession of stocks and bonds in addition to the relative dividend coupons'. (26) However, since this decree had certain gaps, in June 1977 the authorities passed two amendments, decree no. 95 and no. 89. These decrees set up a protest system at the stock exchange and the company issuing lost securities and also asked brokers dealing in securities to abide by the rules on the occasion of each sale or purchase of securities.

Later, the authorities decided to organise this protest system so as to make it intelligible to the public. They passed Law no. 28, which stipulates that shares are prohibited from being transacted outside the brokers' ring so as to protect the shareholders' interest, and accepted the Banco Dikona offer to temporarily carry out transactions at its offices.

This move returned confidence to the shareholders, who continued to invest in moveable securities. But, despite the growth in numbers of transactions and increase in prices, especially in certain industrial companies, activities did not reach the level of the 1970-74 period. The reasons for this are largely due to the fact that 'millions of pounds of shares, most of them bearer stocks, were lost, burned or stolen during the war'. (27) The negative effects were also felt in the absence of authentic information from quoted companies which rendered any financial analysis a risky business.

Due to the deteriorating political situation, the stock exchange closed down in 1978. It re-opened again in mid-1979, when the number of transactions reached 66,546 while their monetary value reached LL 24.7 million, a noticeable rise on that of 1977 due to people selling off their shares in fear of the Israeli-Lebanese war of 1978. The number of transactions went on declining to reach 18,788 in 1980, 7,037 in 1981, 33,795 in 1982 and 27,117 in 1983 while their monetary value reached LL 1.9 million 654.8 thousands, LL 2.5 million and LL 2.1 million respectively. There is no further data on the stock exchange since 1983. However, it is known to either have dropped dramatically or stopped completely due to the prevailing security situation. (See Table 3.7).

NOTES

1.   Agtmael, A. (1984) Emerging securities market, London: Euromoney Publications, p. 164.
2.   Jordan Central Bank (1978) Fifteenth Annual Report, p. 49.
3.   'Stock exchange off to fast start' (1978) Financial Times, 6 July.
4.   Jordan Central Bank (1978) Fifteenth Annual Report, p. 50.
5.   Industrial Development Bank (1978) Fourteenth Annual Report and Balance Sheet, Jordan, p. 15.
6.   'Stock exchange off to a fast start', (1978) Financial Times, Arab Microfiche Institution, 6 July.
7.   Ibid.
8.   Khouri, R. (1970) 'Activity on stock exchange expected to double this year', Jordan Times, Arab Microfiche Institution, 8 May.
9.   'Stock exchange dealings top $ 17.5m' (1979) The Middle East Report, Arab Microfiche Institution, 10 January.
10.   'Stock market trading up 182%' (1980) Middle East Economic Digest, vol. 4, no. 2, January.
11.   Khouri, R. 'Activity on stock exchange expected to double this year' (1979) Jordan Times, Arab Microfiche Institution, 18 May.
12.   'Jordan banking near maturity' (1979) The Middle East, June.
13.   Ibid.
14.   'Bright future for securities business' (1980) Mid East Markets, Arab Microfiche Institution, 14 January.
15.   'Lower fees are welcome news to Amman investors' (1983) Middle East Economic Digest, vol. 27, no. 3, 21 January.
16.   Jordan Central Bank (1981) 18th Annual Report, p. 38.
17.   Jordan Central Bank (1982) 19th Annual Report, p. 41.
18.   Jordan Central Bank (1983) 20th Annual Report, p. 31.
19.   Jordan Central Bank (1985) Twenty Second Annual Report, p. 27.
20.   Jordan Central Bank (1986) Twenty Third Annual Report, p. 26.
21.   Jordan Central Bank (1980) 17th Annual Report,

p. 35.

22.   Jordan Central Bank (1982) 19th Annual Report, pp. 39-40.

23.   Ibid, p. 40.

24.   'Beirut Exchange idle for a day' (1966) Egyptian Gazette, Arab Microfiche Institution, 5 February.

25.   Association of Banks in Lebanon (1972) Annual Report, 23 March.

26.   Khawaja, A. (1979) 'Stock exchange: industrial shares represent 70% of total transactions' Arab Economist, no. 104, May.

27.   'Beirut stock exchange re-opens' (1977) IKE, Arab Microfiche Institution, 7 September.

Chapter Four

STOCK MARKETS IN ARAB AFRICAN COUNTRIES

I   THE EGYPTIAN STOCK MARKET

A   Historical background (1883-1980)

Egypt's stock exchanges, Alexandria and Cairo, are the oldest in the Arab world, having being set up in 1883 and 1890 respectively. The Cairo Stock Exchange was established by the British as a base for their merchants. By 1906, the joint stock companies traded in the exchange amounted to 328 with a total capital of LE 91 million. In 1933 a stock exchange law was adopted, to be revised in 1957 and 1959. The Egyptian economy gained from the creation of a considerable number of joint stock companies which helped meet the country's demand during the Second World War. As a result 'Egypt had witnessed a strong and flourishing private sector and an active capital market'. (1)

Activities on both the Cairo and Alexandria exchanges were relatively active, with a daily volume of transactions exceeding LE 1 million, until 1958, the year of the Egyptian and Syrian union. During 1958, 227 companies were listed with a share trading volume reaching LE 66.7 million. Also, 'some eleven government bonds and 18 non-government bonds and about 290 joint venture stocks of a total nominal value of about LE 500 million, were all registered on the two stock markets'. (2) When President Nasser began to nationalise the Egyptian economy at the beginning of the 1960s, the stock exchanges were left undisturbed, though only 55 companies remained listed with a trading volume ranging between LE 3 to 7 million per year. Circulation of governmental and non-governmental bonds dropped to only eight. Interestingly enough, the government subsidised those brokers whose brokerage commissions dropped to nil. This shift towards a centralised planned economy and state ownership 'of private sector enterprises resulted in a total stagnation of the private sector and a complete loss of confidence on the part of private savers in investing in the securities market'. (3)

Interest in creating a more active capital market in Egypt began in 1973, after President Sadat introduced the 'open-door' economic policy. This new policy 'began with a major campaign launched by the Egyptian government, inviting residents and non-resident Egyptian, Arabs and foreign capital to co-operate in exploiting any available resources in the country'. (4) To stimulate private sector development after many years of public sector domination, law no. 43 was amended in 1974 to facilitate the establishment of new joint investment companies between Egyptians and foreign investors, with major tax exemptions and guarantees. As such, licences were given to foreign banks which opened up purely on an offshore basis, and whose role was limited to taking foreign currency deposits and did not interfere in the purely domestic currency markets. Licences were also given to those banks who participated in domestic business but only after more than 50 per cent of the operation was controlled by Egyptians.

Proposals to enlarge and develop the stock exchange were discussed in 1975 at a meeting attended by representatives of the stock exchange, the banks and some of the officials concerned with Egypt's financial affairs. After further discussions, it was decided to appoint a working committee to co-ordinate ideas in a unified proposal which dealt with two aspects - the activation and the development of the stock exchange.

The aims behind the development of the stock exchange were to 'make Cairo an international finance centre in accordance with President Sadat's directive' (5) so as to mobilise reources and channel them to long-term investment needed for economic recovery. They were also concerned with the reform of the stock exchange administration and the brokers, as well as with the introduction of new equipment and scientific and technological devices which the International Finance Corporation promised to offer.

Another conference in 1976 looked into the possibilities of creating a money and capital market. The deputy governor of the Egyptian Central Bank, Dr Banna, announced that reforms were being considered in the face of the deficient exchange rate policy and exchange control system. This reform would bring a boost to economic activities by 'minimising regulations and restrictions on holding and using foreign exchange, encouraging the transfer to Egypt of Egyptian savings held abroad, boosting foreign investment and foreign bank deposits in Egypt and starting a free currency market for the Egyptian pound'. (6)

Although some members were doubtful that the reform would be introduced in time, or that the resources of the central bank would be enough to carry it through, Dr Banna assured them that the new banking law of 1975, which gave the centre bank the flexibility to restore equilibrium in interest rate levies and which also gave commercial banks the freedom to deal with any economic sector - which previously they were not allowed to do - would enable the central bank to be part of the development proposals.

As a result of such moves, a number of foreign banks have moved into Egypt. However, a number of obstacles remain. Banks with offshore licences, which attracted the Egyptians because it was thought that these would create a financial centre in Cairo and open the way to financing of important projects by drawing on their foreign currency resources, were reluctant to commit any funds for domestic projects. Joint ventures proved to be more active in the domestic market, but these committed sums of money only to operations which they could control themselves.

Stock market reactions to the open-door policy have been encouraging. Transactions which were dormant before increased, and what few bonds and shares existed increased their market prices. Although total transactions in company shares declined in 1977 by 14 per cent and their normal value by 13 per cent - while their market price fell by 5 per cent compared with 1976 - they rose again to 20.9 per cent with a nominal value of 19.8 per cent and a market value of 6.7 per cent in 1978. In 1979, total transactions again declined by 9.6 per cent in number of shares, by 6 per cent in nominal value and with an increase of 1.6 per cent in market value.

The total volume of transactions, shares and bonds, in 1977 declined by 27.6 per cent in number, by 41 per cent in nominal value and by 35 per cent at market price, compared with 1976; in 1978 volume increased by 13.9 per cent, the nominal value by 3 per cent and the market value by 2.1 per cent, to further increase by 10.7 per cent, 34 per cent and 3 per cent respectively in 1979.

All this improvement was the result of the decision taken by the stock exchange authorities in 1979 to set up the Capital Market Authority (CMA). This caused optimism on the market as it was hoped that it would revive activities on the stock exchange. The main objectives of the CMA are:

(1) to create, develop and regulate an adequate climate for savings and investments needed for economic development;
(2) to promote and develop primary and secondary markets for new and existing issues of all types of financial instruments for providing maximum liquidity;
(3) to foster the recruitment of stock middlemen and provide them with training programmes to raise their professional standards;
(4) to carry out studies and proposals for the government agencies and introduce amendments to the law, to develop and regulate capital markets;
(5) to ensure that the data on securities, issues and brokers are made available to the public;
(6) to ensure that those involved in stock exchange activities are legally licensed and not involved in any exploitation or manipulation.

CMA gave certain groups the job of studying the legal and organisational framework governing the primary and secondary markets. These groups came out with the recommendations for the removal of any impediments by amending the regulations of the market so as to channel savings towards investment in securities.

The recommendations resulted in the CMA issuing three main laws in 1981. With regard to the general regulations for the stock exchange, the CMA suggested the adoption of the correspondent members system, which allows foreign brokers to be listed at the Egyptian stock exchanges, in exchange for Egyptian members being treated on the same basis; the listing of shares and bonds of foreign companies and stocks in foreign currency at the Egyptian stock exchanges; the forming of brokerage firms jointly, by foreign and Egyptian brokers.

The new companies law sets down that the establishment of a company requires the approval of a committee of specialised technical members instead of the Minister; the law protects small savers; and sets down the rules for the establishment of companies dealing in securities, by underwriting the public offering and re-offering it for public subscription.

The income tax law exempted shares and bonds from: tax previously set on the dividends of companies' shares amounting to 40 per cent of the coupons; interest tax on bonds issued by Egyptian joint stock companies, whether public or private, for the amount not to exceed the interest rates set by the Central Bank on deposits with banks; the general income tax in amount up to 30 per cent of the taxable income within a maximum limit of LE 3,000 if such amounts are invested in securities, in long-term deposits and in investment certificates.

B **Development and activities (1980–1986)**

There was an increase in stock transactions in 1980, both in nominal value of 64 per cent and market value of 65 per cent, while the number of transacted securities declined by 3.2 per cent. The dealings in foreign investment shares registered on the stock exchange resulted in an increase in the total volume of transactions. There was also an increase of 15.5 per cent in the number of shares and 30.8 per cent of the nominal value and 227.3 per cent of the market value.

However, the number of transactions in government bonds decreased by 39.3 per cent and declined in nominal value by 43.6 per cent and market value by 50 per cent. This was due to a decline in the average price per bond to LE 6 against LE 8.7 in 1979.

> This decrease is attributed to the drop in the number of bonds in circulation, these being confined to dollar development bonds and Al-Djihad bonds in Egyptian pounds which have not been of much interest to the public owing to their low yield compared with other savings channels. (7)

Developments in 1980 show that the volume of transactions in companies' shares increased to LE 1,036,382 at market value. This increase was accompanied by a decline in the prices of most shares because of 'excessive sale orders in completion of liquidation operations' (8) and the unwillingness of investors to buy because of the large difference between stock dividends compared with interest rates of other savings channels. The decline was most noticeable in share prices of industrial and building sectors, while share prices of spinning and weaving companies fluctuated. In February, the volume of transactions declined by 83 per cent because of the continued increase in sale orders and the fall in purchase orders which caused most share prices to decline, with the exception of a limited number of company shares in housing which improved due to more purchase orders. The number of transactions further increased in April because shares of a new foreign investment company (Misr Iran Hotels Company) issued in foreign currency were placed on the stock exchange with a market value of 3,071,500, 'and in addition to the state of optimism prevailing in the market because of shareholders' expectations regarding larger distribution profits than the previous year'. (9) This increase was accompanied by rises in prices of some spinning and weaving companies, while prices of land and building shares stayed stable.

In May and June the volume of transactions experienced another decline of 93.3 per cent at market value of LE 112,886 because of the continued increase in sale orders and the decrease in purchase orders, coupled with the continuing decline in prices of most shares. This was despite the announcement by most companies of larger profits. However, the retainment of a major portion of allocated profits and the huge provisions led to smaller profit distributions to shareholders 'which were in turn reflected in shareholders' reluctance for transactions'. (10) All this, together with raising the structure of interest rates on deposits and investment certificates by 2 per cent, affected market activity.

In July and August the volume of transactions in company shares increased to a market value of LE 140,768. This increase was because transactions in some companies were dominated by foreign currencies. At the same time, purchase orders for shares ceased for companies whose balance sheets showed a decline in distributed profits which, in turn, led to a decline in their share prices. An increase in share prices was witnessed by companies with better profits, such as spinning, weaving and mortgage companies, because of new purchase orders that absorbed sale offers. The volume of transactions continued in flux between a decrease and increase during the last months of 1980. A low price level is considered to encourage share purchases because it increases the yield of shares. Low prices did prevail, 'yet purchase orders were not responsive because shareholders were awaiting the results of draft companies law, and also draft taxation laws, on which dealings would depend'. (11)

Regarding the volume of transactions in government bonds during 1980, we notice a decline of 74 per cent at market value, accompanied by a decline of 4.5 per cent in prices in Al-Djihad bonds because sale orders were higher than purchase orders, while dollar development bonds improved because of increased purchase orders. In January transactions in dollar development bonds represented 68.5 per cent of total volume of transactions in government bonds, to double in February due to more orders for the purchase of development bonds after the decrease in their market price. This meant that dealings in dollar development bonds increased to 95 per cent of total transactions in government bonds. Purchase orders for Al-Djihad bonds also increased by 4.5 per cent as some private sector companies decided to invest 5 per cent of their net profits in government bonds in compliance with law no. 7 of 1959. In March, the volume of transactions fell by 10 per cent because of the reduction in prices of dollar development bonds and Al-Djihad bonds, to reach its highest peak in April at market value of 206,536.

This increase in demand for dollar development bonds, 94.4 per cent of total transactions in bonds, 'was due to increased purchase orders from private sector companies to invest 5 per cent of their net profits in development bonds since their return is comparatively higher than government bonds in Egyptian pounds.' (12)

In July the volume of transactions in government bonds decreased in market value by 53 per cent due to a halt in the previous trend taken by private companies accompanied by the stability of Al-Djihad bonds, at 4.5 per cent. The volume of transactions for both bonds rose by 140 per cent in August to decline again in September and October. In December the volume for both bonds decreased by 83.3 per cent 'because of lower purchase orders in anticipation of high interest rates on deposits and investment certificates at the beginning of 1981'. (13)

In the first quarter of 1981, the total volume of transactions decreased by 55 per cent at market value and 52 per cent at nominal value, while the number of securities increased by 10.7 per cent, to decrease in the second quarter in both number and nominal value by 6 per cent and 4.6 per cent respectively, while market value increased by

210.2 per cent.

Transactions in company shares of both market and nominal values decreased by 79 per cent and 82 per cent respectively, while in the second quarter they increased by 9.7 per cent and 158 per cent respectively. At the same time, the volume of transactions in government bonds at both market and nominal values increased by 46.3 per cent and 68.8 per cent respectively, while in the second quarter it decreased by 36.9 per cent and 39.1 per cent respectively.

The total volume of transactions in company shares during the first quarter of 1981 reveals a decline in both nominal and market values of 52 per cent and 60 per cent respectively, for the market value to increase in the second quarter by 51 per cent while nominal value further decreased by 68.2 per cent. All this indicates that transactions were centred around low nominal value shares.

By comparison, the volume of transactions in government bonds reached LE 311,324 at market value. This was coupled with an increase in prices of dollar development bonds 'due to the appearance of purchase orders for 95 per cent of transactions, as the real return is almost equal to interest rates on bank deposits in foreign currencies'. (14)

During the first quarter of 1981 the total volume of transactions in government bonds reveals an increase of 136.1 per cent in number and 125.4 per cent at market value, despite the decline in the average market value per bond to LE 5.7, while in the second quarter it further increased by 22 per cent and 26 per cent respectively, with an increase in the average market value per bond to LE6.

Law no. 121 of 1981 amended the general regulations of the stock exchange to allow for more flexibility that would encourage new investment companies to quote their shares on the market. Law no. 157 related to income taxes and law no. 159 to joint stock companies. Although it was thought that these laws would stimulate the stock market and end the state of recession, 'the market remained rather quiet as the benefits of the new laws were still unknown to a number of dealers and their impact on the market might be felt after the announcement of dividends'. (15) Also, most shares that were being circulated were of joint public sector companies which would not benefit from these laws.

The year 1982 was characterised by a decline in company shares and government bonds denominated in Egyptian pounds by 73.3 per cent at market value and 13.6 per cent in number. Transactions in dollar denominated securities increased by 31.7 per cent at market value to reach $4.2 million, while sterling denominations decreased by 82 per cent to reach £21.5 thousand.

Transactions in government bonds in Egyptian pounds decreased by 69.3 per cent at market value because of the fewer bonds in circulation after the redemption of the Al-Djihad bonds with a nominal value of LE 35 million with a low yield of 4.5 per cent compared with other savings channels. Further decline in dealings was expected after the issuing of law no. 159 which had abolished the commitment to invest 5 per cent of net profits in government bonds. By contrast, the total volume of transactions in dollar-denominated Egyptian government bonds increased by 28.1 per cent at market value. This was the result of heavier purchase orders, due to the decline in their market value and consequently the rise in their real return, considering the difference between the market value and the redemption value.

While the volume of dealings in company shares denominated in Egyptian pounds decreased by 73.4 per cent at market value and 12 per cent in number, transactions in dollar-denominated shares increased by 191.5 per cent to reach $201.2 thousand at market value; volume of transactions in shares of sterling denomination declined to £21.5 thousand. The decline in dealings in Egyptian pound shares was due to fewer purchase orders, since returns had declined, causing investors to prefer bank deposits, which yield larger interests.

Transactions in shares of Egyptian pound denomination showed a decrease of 69.4 per cent in market value to reach LE 408 thousand, and of 24.3 per cent in number of shares to reach 175 thousand shares. Accompanying this was a decline in most company shares, particularly industrial shares. Transactions in dollar-denominated company shares fell to $3.4 thousand at market value to further increase to $160 thousand at the end of 1982. This increase is attributed to an increase in the number of shares denominated in foreign currencies and quoted on the stock exchange: 18 new companies were registered in March 1982, and 13 in June 1982.

The year 1983 showed promising activities in the stock exchange, where dealings in denominated Egyptian pounds, both government bonds and company shares, increased in number and value by 72.4 per cent and 249.2 per cent respectively. Also, transactions in securities of dollar and sterling denominations increased by 193.2 per cent and 35.9 per cent respectively.

The returns of the stock exchange show an increase in the volume of trading in papers denominated in Egyptian pounds. Those of company shares rose by 73.9 per cent in number. Total dealings at nominal value increased to LE 3.9 million. The increase in the volume of trading was due to more purchase orders being placed after the general improvement of returns on shares. Trading in the shares of dollar and sterling denomination also increased, the former rose in market value to 10.0 million with the average market value per share to $25.4. Also, the nominal value of these papers increased to $5.3 million and the average nominal value per share to 13.3 million. The latter reached £29.3 thousand in market value and the average market value per share was £1.6

By contrast, the volume of transactions in government bonds, both denominated in Egyptian pounds and US dollars, decreased. The decline in dealings in Egyptian pound bonds was LE 46 at market value because transactions were limited to Al-Djihad bonds.

Dealings in dollar development bonds fell to $2.3 millions, despite the rise in the average market value per bond to $9. The reason for this is that 'purchased orders surpassed the number of sale orders as holders had been inclined to retain these bonds for their higher real yields as compared with the prevailing interest rates on dollar deposits'. (16)

The volume of dealings in securities denominated in both Egyptian pounds and US dollars showed a large improvement during 1984. The volume of transactions in Egyptian pound securities (government bonds and company shares) increased by 43.3 per cent to reach LE 9.125 thousand pounds at market value. The market value of dollar denominated securities increased by 80.4 per cent, while the volume of trading in sterling denominations at market value declined by 94.9 per cent to reach £1,500.

The volume of transactions in company shares denominated in Egyptian pounds increased by 106.6 per cent in number and by 289.3 per cent in nominal value. The average nominal value per share rose to LE 4.3, thus increasing the total volume to transactions at nominal value by 92.8 per cent to 5,560.9 thousands. As regards the average market value per share, the increase amounted to LE 6.9. This shows that dealings concentrated in company shares with higher nominal value. Increased purchase orders for shares of mixed sector companies, whose budget showed improvements in the distribution of profits, resulted in higher prices. Shares of private sector companies continued to be in demand, especially after their balance sheets showed larger distributable profits.

Around 32 new Egyptian joint stock companies were registered in the stock exchange during 1983-4, 14 of which are closed companies whose capital is not offered for public subscription.

The volume of transactions in US dollar shares increased at market value to reach US $21.3 million, while the average market value per share dropped by 16.1 per cent to 21.3. The expansion was 'not only due to marriage transactions but also to expansion demand balance of increased levels of profit distribution and a rise in transactions in shares of high value'. (17)

Transactions in dollar development bonds declined by 59.4 per cent to US $821.6 thousand at market value, while the average price per share rose to $9.3. The decline in the volume of transactions is 'attributed to an increase in real yield due to approaching maturities since all issues of these bonds will be redeemed between December 1984 and July 1985'. (18)

As for government bonds of Egyptian pound denomination, dealings began on housing bonds which were the only bonds circulating in local currency on the stock exchange. The volume of transactions at market value amounted to LE 315.9 thousand, against a nominal value of LE 602.7 thousand. The sharp decline in the market value compared with the nominal value is due to their maturities coupled with their low interest rate.

During 1985 the volume of dealings in securities denominated in both Egyptian pounds and US dollars continued to improve. The volume of transactions in Egyptian pounds securities - government bonds and company shares - increased by 121.8 per cent compared with the previous year, to reach LE 20.237 thousand pounds at market value against LE 9.125 thousand in 1984. The market value of dollar-denominated securities increased by 263.9 per cent to reach $39.405 thousand in 1985 against $10.829 thousand in 1984, while the volume of trading in sterling denominations at market value increased by 23.3 per cent to reach £1.850.

The volume of transactions in company shares

denominated in Egyptian pounds increased by 142.8 per cent in nominal value and by 72.2 per cent in number. The average nominal value per share rose to LE 6, thus increasing the total volume of transactions at market value by 116.7 per cent to LE 19.458 thousand in 1985 as against LE 8.980 in 1984. The average market value per share increased to LE 8.6. This improvement in operations was due to increased purchase orders for mixed company shares and to an increase in the number of joint stock companies registered at the stock exchange, whose number reached 266 companies in 1985.

The volume of transactions in US dollar shares increased at market value by 290.2 per cent and at nominal value by 365.4 per cent, while the average market value per share declined by 20.3 per cent to $15.7

Transactions in dollar-denominated bonds declined by 57.9 per cent and 56.8 per cent respectively to $374.560 at nominal value and $354.606 at market value. On the other hand, the average market value per share rose by 3.3 per cent to $9.5. The decline 'is attributed to the fact that holders of these bonds prefer to retain them in view of their close maturity dates'. (19)

During this period, dealing in Egyptian pound government bonds was also confined to housing bonds. The volume of transactions in these bonds increased by 338.6 per cent both in value and in number, while the average market value per share increased by 20 per cent.

In 1986 the volume of dealings in securities denominated in Egyptian pounds declined by 1.9 per cent at market value due to a decline in dealings in company shares and an increase in dealings in government bonds. On the other hand, dealings in securities denominated in US dollars increased by 74.9 per cent while dealings in securities denominated in sterling declined by 63.5 per cent to reach £675.

The volume of transactions in company shares denominated in Egyptian pounds declined by 2.3 per cent in nominal value and increased by 12.9 per cent in number. The average nominal value per share declined by 14 per cent to reach LE 4.9 in 1986 against LE 6 in 1985, while the average market value per share declined by 13.4 per cent to reach LE 7.1 in 1986 as against LE 8.6 in 1985, thus leading to a 2.2 per cent decline in the volume of dealings at market value.

Company shares of US dollar denominations rose by

95

Table 4.1: Activities of the Cairo stock exchange: volume of transactions for government bonds 1980–1986 (in millions)

Year	1980	1981	1982	1983	1984	1985	1986
A In Egyptian pounds							
Quantity	.095	.0157	.008	.005	.603	1.702	1.613
Nominal value	.697	.157	.079	.05	.603	1.702	1.613
Market value	.630	.141	.077	.046	.316	1.106	1.164
B In US dollars $							
Quantity	.073	.127	.461	.257	.101	.045	.016
Nominal value	.0734	1.300	4.600	2.570	1.010	.447	.159
Market value	.0572	1.130	4.000	2.310	.940	.422	.169

Source: Central Bank of Egypt, Annual Report, various issues

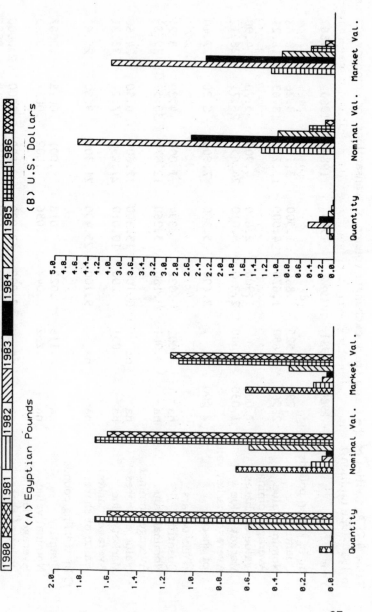

Figure 4.1: Activities of Cairo stock exchange: volume of transactions for government bonds in millions 1980-1986

(A) Egyptian Pounds

(B) U.S. Dollars

Table 4.2: Activities of the Cairo stock exchange: volume of transactions for company shares in 1980-1986 (millions)

Year	1980	1981	1982	1983	1984	1985	1986
A In Egyptian pounds							
Quantity	.294	.525	.866	1.500	3.110	3.26	3.68
Nominal value	2.560	3.690	1.670	4.000	15.270	18.63	18.21
Average nominal value of shares	7.000	na	1.900	2.600	4.900	5.70	4.90
Market value	1.030	4.000	2.210	8.010	24.650	26.71	26.12
Average market value of shares	2.500	na	2.600	5.300	7.900	8.20	7.10
B In US dollars							
Quantity	na	.002	.022	.394	1.000	4.80	3.24
Nominal value	na	.061	.180	5.260	12.670	30.50	79.80
Average nominal value of shares	na	na	8.100	13.300	12.600	6.30	24.60
Market value	na	.051	.200	10.010	21.290	47.24	83.21
Average market value of shares	na	na	9.100	25.400	21.300	9.80	25.60
C In sterling pounds							
Quantity	na	.116	.022	.018	.001	.0018	.0007
Nominal value	na	.232	.044	.036	.002	.0037	.0015
Average nominal value of shares	na	na	2.000	2.000	2.000	2.0000	2.0000
Market value	na	.116	.022	.029	.0015	.0018	.0006
Average market value of shares	na	na	1.000	1.600	1.500	1.0000	0.9000

98

Source: Central Bank of Egypt, Annual Report, various issues

Figure 4.2: Activities of the Cairo stock exchange: volume of transactions (millions) for company shares ('N' means not available)

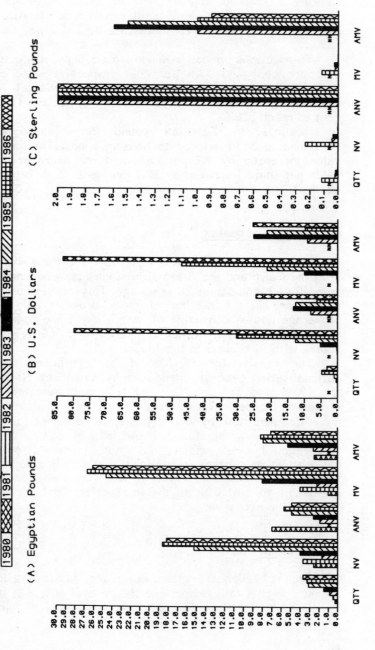

(A) Egyptian Pounds   (B) U.S. Dollars   (C) Sterling Pounds

161.6 per cent in their nominal value during 1986, thus showing a marked improvement in the average nominal value per share by 290.5 per cent to reach $24.6. Also, the average market value per share rose by 161.2 per cent to $25.6.

Transactions in dollar-denominated bonds declined by 64.3 per cent and 59.9 per cent respectively, to reach $159.580 at nominal value and $160.329 at market value. The average market value per share dropped by 11.6 per cent to reach $10.6

Dealings in Egyptian pound denominated bonds continued to be restricted to housing bonds. Their market value increased by 5.2 per cent and the average market value per share improved by 10.8 per cent. (See Tables 4.1 and 4.2).

C Methods of dealing

As many as 113 joint stock companies trade their shares in both the Cairo and the Alexandria stock markets, compared with 50 such companies 20 years ago. This increase parallels a decrease in the number of stock brokers: only seven brokerage houses consisting of nine brokers are conducting deals at the present time, compared with 46 brokerage houses with 61 brokers in the 1950s.

The reason for this could be attributed to the nationalisation process introduced by President Nassar in the 1950s and 1960s, which led to the closure of some brokerage houses. Those brokers who lost their earnings were compensated by the Ministry of Finance and the central bank, which found them jobs in banks. As for brokerage houses which did not close after the nationalisation process, the Ministry of Finance supported these. Their number, however, is still very small and they are unable to deal with all the transactions that are taking place on the exchange.

D Problems

(1) Lack of adequate information and audited financial statements to investors and the general public as these are not published regularly to allow shareholders to assess performances accurately.

(2) The brokerage system lacks disciplined brokers with the knowledge and training to direct shareholders and initiate stock. In addition, the number of brokers is small, totalling only nine brokers in both markets.
(3) The use of speculation by dealers in order to make quick profits.
(4) The world economic recession which resulted in the decline of revenues of Arab oil producing countries, coupled with rejection by these countries of Egypt after the Camp David accord was signed, which in turn cut down the financial assistance from these countries.
(5) Both the Cairo and Alexandria markets suffer from a shares shortage.
(6) The narrowness of the domestic base for investment.
(7) The establishment of shareholding companies that do not take into account the needs of the economy as they are competitive and tend to direct investment in the wrong sectors.

II THE MOROCCAN STOCK MARKET

The Moroccan securities' market dates back to 1929 when the leading banks of Casablanca set up the Office de Compensation 'to allow trading largely by French expatriates, in local companies which were not listed in the Paris Bourse'. (20) In 1948 this was replaced by the Office de Cotation de Valeurs Mobilieres, which worked like a local stock exchange with three, and later five, sessions per week. Activity grew steadily and peaked in 1955 just before independence, an event which had a terrible effect on trading volume and prices.

In 1967, a royal decree abrogated the statute of the Office de Cotation de Valeurs Mobilieres and formed the Casablanca Stock Exchange, patterned on the Paris Bourse. Another royal decree set out the rules for regulating the secondary market activities under the supervision of the Finance Ministry which was represented through a commissioner on the exchange, while the primary market remained unregulated.

Organisation and function
As we said earlier, the stock exchange is supervised by the Minister of Finance, who appoints a government

commissioner, whose responsibility is to make sure that transactions are legal. In addition to his advisory functions, he has veto power on decisions as to which securities are to be admitted to quotation. The conduct of the bourse's affairs is in the hands of the board of directors, the technical committee and the managing director.

Stockbrokers have the right of transaction in listed securities and others traded on the stock exchange, in addition to the registration of direct deals. The Minister of Finance appoints brokers after advice from the technical committee. In addition to being 'directly responsible for the legality of their transactions, and may not buy or sell on their own account, they have to lodge with the Treasury depositing in cash or securities as coverage for all their commitments'. (21)

Stockbrokers may be individuals or companies. If individuals, they must be over 30 years of age and of Moroccan nationality. If brokerage companies, they must be either a limited liabilities company or a limited partnership with a capital of 50,000 dirhams. All 14 brokers authorised by the Casablanca Stock Exchange are banking institutions with no participation from individual brokers.

Daily sessions are held on the exchange, except for public holidays. Prices are restricted in the sense that they must not vary by more than 5 per cent from one session to the next, 'which may affect the negotiability of securities and may make stock exchange prices less representative'. (22) As for the nature of transactions, direct deals are permissible and not prohibited by the authorities.

Dealing in the secondary market takes place in five separate market compartments which have different roles. Some deal with listed securities, others with those not listed, while still others with dealings neither listed nor traded on any of the markets.

Whereas government and government guaranteed stocks and mortgage bonds are admitted to quotation as of right, other securities, such as corporate bonds and shares, are admitted to quotation by decision of the bourse committee after meeting the following requirements:

(1) a company's balance sheet and reports for the last three years;
(2) a company should supply information on its past performance and its future plans;
(3) a company should submit a list of its directors and

shareholders.

Another major listing requirement for the applicant company is to offer to the public shares of at least 20 per cent of its authorised capital. All in all, these rules are similar to rules in other countries, if it was not for the requirement that shares should be issued at a price well below their perceived value, which impedes the development of the market. In addition, the small size of the Moroccan companies and the reluctance of most entrepreneurs to include outsiders among the shareholders limits the growth of supply of stocks. Nevertheless, trading in the equity market between the years 1967-76 expanded, but declined after that, since there have been hardly any new issues, to reach DH 57.5 million in 1982 as against DH 209.5 million in 1975.

The secondary market was affected as well in the pre-1976 years, when the volume of business fell drastically. The reasons for this were the use of speculation which kept savers away from the markets. Another was the decision by the authorities to raise the short-term interest rates which resulted in a 'negative differential compared with the average yield of quoted shares, and people found they could get better returns by putting their money in bank and non-bank deposits'. (23) In addition to these factors, the lack of tax incentives to go public paralysed the stock exchange.

Following the stagnation between 1976 and 1982, a revival in stock exchange activity took place in 1983, but with modest levels of indices and of turnover. The volume of transactions amounted to DH 152 million and direct transfers expanded by 7 per cent due to the increase in the number of holdings acquired by companies in other enterprises. Activity in the equity sector which was slack for several years expanded substantially in the middle of the 1980s because of the introduction of 87,000 new shares.

A considerable change was also noticed in the structure of dealings, with fixed-interest securities, at less than 10 million dirhams, accounting for 6 per cent of total turnover. Also, dealings in shares increased by 19 per cent to reach DH 140 million, representing 92 per cent of total turnover.

By the end of 1984, the number of listed securities became 22.2 million, an increase of 800,000 over 1983, and stock exchange capitalisation became DH 2252 million compared with DH 2039 million.

The revival of the stock exchange continued in 1985,

stimulated by the listing of two three-year government loans. The volume of stock exchange dealings expanded by 47.1 per cent to reach DH 22 3.6 million in 1985 as against DH 152 million in 1984. Improvement was most noticeable in the market for fixed interest securities dominated by government securities, while share dealings decreased by 10 per cent from DH 140 to 126.3 million.

The predominant form of trading remained direct sales, with a volume of transactions of DH 127.7 million, due to new buyers wishing to obtain control of certain companies. Purchases of government securities were made mainly by insurance companies. The increase in the capital of companies already listed resulted in an increase in the number of listed variable-yield securities.

III THE TUNISIAN STOCK MARKET

Creation of the Tunisian stock market and its function

Proposals for the establishment of a Tunisian financial market were discussed in the ten-year development plan after independence. The government took the initiative in preparing loans and government bonds, to be issued in 1957, 1964, 1973 and 1975 respectively. Also, the government controlled the giving of loans, whether to the private sector or to others.

Later on, the need for a financial market became urgent due to the stability and activity of the national economy. As a result, the earlier proposals and initiatives played a part in giving birth to the idea of a stock exchange, which came into being during a national seminar on savings. However, it was not until 1969 that a Tunisian stock exchange was set up.

The following points were put forward in defining the aims of the stock exchange:

(1) to facilitate and organise the securities market;
(2) to find the proper method for enacting the activities;
(3) to facilitate new capital by companies;
(4) to encourage the mobilisation and investment of capital in securities.

By law, the stock exchange was able to arrange for securities to be made at the stock exchange and through stock brokers. 'This rule of centralisation was intended not only to invigorate the stock exchange, but also to restore order to the secondary market where speculation had been rife, to the detriment of less sagacious investors.' (24)

Regulating and supervising the stock exchange is the responsibility of the Minister of Finance. He appoints the bourse members and a government commissioner. The bourse committee and its chairman are responsible for managing the stock exchange and conducting its affairs. The committee's other job is to advise and 'after due examination of requests for listing, decide what securities are to be admitted to quotation'. (25)

Stockbrokers are the only authorised body to deal on the stock exchange. Their responsibility lies in settling transactions, furnishing appropriate financial guarantees and ensuring the exercise of their profession against risks. Finally, they must keep regular accounts and register with the stockbrokers' association.

Another function of the Tunisian stock exchange concerns the laws of brokerage. As there are few private individuals with the necessary financial resources, and as the volume of business is so small, most brokers are financial institutions. The reason behind the banks' role in the financial market is because they 'do have a sound financial basis and trained staff they certainly are best able to act as brokers'. (26)

Tunisian law is vague regarding the control and organisation of the new issue market. No-one has the means to intervene for co-ordinating and controlling the flow of funds through the capital market. Also, the transacted securities are limited in the hands of a few selected individuals who prefer to take care of the sale of their securities to the public themselves. Modern issuing techniques and mechanisms are lacking, thus preventing the growth of volume of new issues. Issuers do not sell to the public but turn to the banks for help.

Another adverse factor in the issue market is the structure of capital supply and demand. The state, two public corporations, and three financial intermediaries exclusively float bond issues. On the other hand, industrial enterprises and private sector companies prefer bank loans and indirect medium and long-term borrowing.

As for the equity market, it has its own problems too. New shares are hardly ever offered to the public and to prevent the entry of new shareholders, companies stipulate that their shares may be sold only subject to approval by the board of directors or reserve themselves a priority right in share purchase. As such, many companies prefer to retain profit rather than distribute it as dividends. This irregularity of dividends is encouraged by the tax system which 'favours capital increases by means of capitalization of reserves'. (27)

In short, the new Tunisian issue market is small and disorganised, it gets funds from institutional investors, and it lacks both issuers and specialists in placing and managing securities.

Coupled with this, there are 48 securities listed in the market which together combine to restrict the volume of stock exchange transactions. Around 70 per cent of stock exchange transactions are in non-listed securities traded on the secondary market while 30 per cent are for the primary market.

NOTES

1. 'Securities and mobilization of saving in Egypt' (1982) Investment Review, vol. 3, no. 2.
2. Sabbagh, N. (1976) 'The revival of the Egyptian stock market', Euromoney, March.
3. 'Securities and mobilization of saving in Egypt' (1982) Investment Review, vol. 3, no. 2.
4. Sabbagh, N. (1976) 'The revival of the Egyptian stock market', Euromoney, March.
5. 'Ministry IFC study stock exchange' (1975) Egyptian Mail, Arab Microfiche Institution, 6 December.
6. Field, P. (1976) 'Egypt needs capital market', Financial Times, Arab Microfiche Institute, 10 June.
7. Egypt Central Bank (1980) Annual Report, p. 29.
8. Ibid., p. 29.
9. Egypt Central Bank (1980) Economic Review, vol. XX, no. 1, p. 165.
10. Ibid. p. 165.
11. Egypt Central Bank (1980) Economic Review, vol. XX, nos 3 and 4, p. 268.
12. Egypt Central Bank (1980) Annual Report, p. 30.
13. Egypt Central Bank (1980) Economic Review, vol. XX, nos 3 and 4, p. 269.
14. Egypt Central Bank (1981) Economic Review, vol. xxi, no. 1, p. 57.

15.   Egypt Central Bank (1981) <u>Economic Review</u>, vol. xxi, nos 3 and 4, pp. 262-3.
16.   Egypt Central Bank (1983) <u>Annual Report</u>, p. 65.
17.   Egypt Central Bank (1984) <u>Economic Review</u>, vol. xxiv, no. 1, p. 56.
18.   Egypt Central Bank (1984) <u>Annual Report</u>, p. 74.
19.   Egypt Central Bank (1985) <u>Economic Review</u>, vol. XXV, no. 1, p. 62.
20.   Agtmael, A. (1984) <u>Emerging securities market</u>, London: Euromoney Publications, p. 182.
21.   Calamanti, A. (1983) <u>The securities market and underdevelopment</u>, Milan: Giuffre Publishers, p. 142.
22.   Ibid. p. 144.
23.   Ibid. p. 170.
24.   Ibid. p. 186.
25.   Ibid. p. 187.
26.   Ibid. p. 187.
27.   Ibid. p. 195.

Chapter Five

PROSPECTS AND PROBLEMS FOR THE REGIONAL INTEGRATION OF ARAB CAPITAL MARKETS

I   INTRODUCTION

There are three principal types of long-term capital exports: private, direct and portfolio investment abroad; economic aid to developing nations; and issue of foreign securities in the capital markets of member countries.

Although the first two have already been applied, the third has not. Arab investment in foreign securities has risen in the last few years, conducted mainly in America and Western Europe. As for the aid channelled through development finance institutions, 'It can be noted that over the past ten years these institutions have given 415 loans to Arab countries, with a total amount of 6.3 billion dollars.' (1) The third, floating securities for foreign issuers on the national capital markets, seems to present more difficulties.

In the past, Arab countries have been geared toward the motto 'lending money is easier than investing it'. This is because advancing funds for a fixed rate of return, independent of whatever the achievements of enterprise being financed, has always been a safer bet than putting the same amount of money in and taking your chances on the outcome. This view, along with ensuring an absence of risk capital, has kept the Arab world in a state of economic decline since many investment outlets were not being used to their full capacity. As such, liquidity and safety have been the two principal determinants of most Arab oil-surplus countries' investment policies.

The policy of directing part of the resources of surplus Arab countries to the capital needy-Arab countries has been reflected since 1967 in the official grants to countries suffering from losses in foreign exchange earnings. It has also been evident in lending in support of development projects and loans made to some countries to relieve exchange difficulties or to finance essential imports.

During the 1970s there was a rapid increase in the number of development funds or banks where Arab oil-producing countries saw the need to commit part of their financial surpluses into long-term development projects in the rest of the Arab world. These surplus countries came to realise the need to 'take an active role in developing the productive facilities of the region rather than merely to be money lenders'. (2)

The most significant form of direct investment was the establishment of joint ventures in the form of lending companies, owning shares, and participation in regional enterprises, or in operating levels. This being said, only Kuwait, unfettered by considerations of oil policy or development spending, has followed freely a course of long-term investment encompassing a more widely diversified range of financial instruments and direct investments than its neighbours. While other Arab oil producers, with a greater domestic absorption capacity and a larger population than Kuwait, did not attempt to follow such a course to the full.

II EVALUATION OF PREVIOUS ATTEMPTS AT INTEGRATION

For the past ten years, the question of the creation of an Arab capital market has been discussed. The reasons for this fusion of various national markets are numerous. Full factor mobility is considered by many experts to be an absolute necessity for efficient allocation of resources. It is argued that since trade and finance are closely interwoven, it is impossible to hand over the former to an international dimension while confining the latter to national dimensions. In an integrated area, borrowers should be given access to credit on equal terms while both loan and equity capital should move freely to places where higher returns can be obtained.

In addition, another argument stresses that the significance of a supranational market goes far beyond the mere fusion of various small markets. Greater size brings with it advantages such as increased efficiency and adaptability and reduced costs. It also ensures the expansion of the investment opportunities of private persons and institutions. The wider the market the better the marketability for securities. On the other hand, from the point of view of demand for capital, an integrated capital market affords a far greater potential than is now available in the separate national markets.

The surplus holders among the Arab countries have a vested interest in the development of security markets in order to extend the domain of their investment opportunities and prevent possible resort to capital controls in the Arab world. Arab net borrowers would benefit from a high degree of security market integration through their increased ability to mobilise Arab savings and through the likely reduction of their borrowing costs resulting from competitive bidding for securities.

Despite the logic of this line of thought, the Arab countries have never made it part of their concept of integration, and have never formulated a concise integration plan. (Nowhere does the Arab League speak of the unification of capital markets as a goal.) This could be seen from historical overviews of Arab plans for integration in general. What the plan does establish is the clearing of decks for the uninhibited movement of capital belonging to residents in member states.

The creation of a wider Arab capital market and an improvement in the functioning of the existing national markets have been included in the agenda. The causes of the inadequacies of the Arab capital markets result from the limited size of the national markets and differences in monetary, fiscal and tax policies. Also, the differential between short and long-term interest rates points to an unusual liquidity preference on the part of the private saving community. It has also been noticed that a large amount of Arab financing includes a large proportion of direct credits, in particular bank credits, as opposed to a smaller proportion of new securities issues. At the same time, institutional investors suffer from rigidities in their investment policy imposed on them by laws and regulations.

These difficulties of the separate national markets in Arab countries make it impossible that they would be able to offer adequate hospitality to a great number of foreign borrowers without endangering their internal equilibrium.

A catalyst for the development of regional capital markets is the establishment of financial structures and institutions through which regional financial transactions can be conducted, 'who would function in environments conducive to the application of their intermediary role'. (3) For the development of national financial institutions in the Arab world is a pre-requisite for the creation of regional financial institutions which, over time, would lead to regional capital integration. Until now, the services of the various capital centres in the Arab world 'have limited their scope to answering local demands for funds and financial services', (4) such as Kuwait, Jordan and Saudi Arabia. These institutions have limited efficiency in their use of the available invested capital. On the other hand, centres such as Lebanon and Bahrain have serviced the international financial markets more than either regional or local financial needs thus draining 'the local and regional environment of the investment capital necessary for funding the expanding economic base of the region'. (5)

Recent developments in the financial markets of the Arab world indicate a strong trend toward the creation of new financial services. Nevertheless, these services, such as funds, banks and development organisations, were the creation of the public sector with little co-operation from the private financial institutions. This trend towards the creation of new funding organisations became more pronounced after the oil boom of 1973 with the accumulation by the Arab oil-exporting countries of financial resources on a very large scale. This brought with it a commitment to the establishment of development finance institutions, to promote the investment of Arab capital within the region. This commitment translated itself into the establishment of several types of institution of a multi-national, national and private nature.

The multi-national institutions created by the Arab League and the Council of Arab Economic Unity to operate on a regional basis include the Arab Fund for Economic and Social Development and the Organisation of Arab Petroleum Exporting Countries (OAPEC). The Arab Fund encouraged private investment as well as emphasizing the development of joint ventures. OAPEC aided the poorest countries in the region by offering interest-free loans with a 20-year maturity and ten-year grace period. Another important institution is the Arab Monetary Fund which was created in 1977 to expand inter-regional trade and further economic development of member countries.

Among the national institutions is the Kuwait Fund for

Arab Economic Development, set up in 1961 to provide development finance. In the 1970s there followed several similar initiatives by Abu Dhabi, Iraq and Saudi Arabia, whose institutions extended long and medium-term loans.

Among private institutions is the Arab Company for Trading Securities (ACTS) which is a private Kuwait-based finance house. 'ACTS is basically a market-making financial institution with a present capacity for spot transactions (in KD bonds and KD certificates of deposit) and tranche accounts, which also provides brokerage and investment services to many private customers and institutions within and outside Kuwait.' (6) ACTS, in consultation with Jordanian Financial Market (JFM) officials, arranged to provide over-the-counter listing and trading services for interested securities currently listed on the JFM. Although this arrangement with JFM securities was found to be workable within Jordanian and Kuwaiti law, as well as according to the rules and regulations of JFM and ACTS, to date not one transaction has taken place. A few practical factors have worked against such an association: (7)

(1) the hesitation of investors in JFM - listed stocks to trade through ACTS because of limitations and delays on the transfer of stock certificates in Jordanian companies;

(2) the small number of interested investors in Jordan-based companies and the paucity of information available to the public about these companies;

(3) the communication problem between Jordan and Kuwait. While ACTS is capable of quoting up-to-the-minute prices for securities traded in New York and Hong Kong for example, it has to wait one or two days for information on stock transactions from the JFM.

The same could be said of the Beirut Stock Market, the Kuwait Stock Exchange and over-the-counter securities market in Bahrain. One reason in such markets for long-term funds is the limited flexibility available to Arab investors in raising investment capital on a regional basis. Whereas international borrowers can float KD bonds in the Kuwait capital market and ensure their marketability by the market-making activity of ACTS, Arab enterprises find it 'impossible to have their debt or equity securities listed, traded or demanded in financial markets other than those of their region'. (8) And whereas it is possible for non-Kuwaiti companies to be listed on the Kuwait Stock Exchange, non-Kuwaiti nationals cannot trade in Kuwait securities. Thus this kind of limitation shows the levels of disintermediation that exists in the region.

III INVESTING ARAB FINANCIAL SURPLUS OUTSIDE THE ARAB REGION

Foreign financial markets, whether Euro or domestic markets, provide a range of opportunities for oil-producing states to invest profitably. The Euro-markets created in the mid-1960s are debt instruments denominated in free currencies issued outside the country's currency of origin and used by governments and international corporations for their borrowing needs. These markets' instruments of debts maturity, range from short - London dollars certificates of deposit, to medium - Euro-credits and long-term Euro-bonds. Investors are interested in these instruments since they are exempted from withholding taxes and foreign exchange restrictions.

The market for London dollar certificates of deposit is narrow and limited and thus is unsuitable for medium and long maturity investment. That is why it is not stable to conduct an investment policy on these certificates. 'The international loans market, or the Euro-currency credits markets is an off-shore bank lending zone whose scope of operations falls outside the range of controls of any of the national monetary or fiscal authorities.' (9) The excess liquidity in various domestic financial systems, such as the slackening domestic credit demand in industrialised countries or accumulated financial surpluses of OPEC countries, enabled the funds to extend credit through this market. Medium-term Euro-credits are met with obstacles which limit their expansion and the growth of their markets. One of these is the narrow capital base of Euro-bonds, as funds deposited with them exceed their ability to manage such funds.

The problem of the Euro-bond market is its narrowness and its dependence on the dollar as the prime currency of issue which renders investment in this market susceptible to the fluctuations in the exchange value of the US dollar. Another shortcoming is the secondary market which does not satisfy the new issues in the primary market because of the absence of capable infrastructures for undertaking dealings in Euro-bonds.

Surplus OPEC funds in the Euro-markets

During the 1970s, a large proportion of surplus oil-fund flows were attracted to the Euro-markets instead of being channelled via the domestic financial markets, despite the view of the greater spread and depth of these which markets can offer. 'The large surpluses accumulated by the Arab oil producers were primarily placed on the same international markets and by-passed the region's commercial demand for funds.' (10)

Flow of OPEC surplus	1974 %
1. Investments in Euro-markets	37
2. Investments in domestic markets	30
3. International agencies	7
4. Other (mainly direct government lending aids and grants)	26
Total	100

Because of the flow of large proportions of surplus oil funds into the international market, a marked revival had been noticed in the major two segments of the Euro-markets, namely Euro-bonds and Euro-credits. International bonds issues figures show 'that new issues for the first seven months of 1975 jumped to $10.2 billion compared with $3.4 billion for 1974'. (11) On the other hand, medium term international bank lending had risen by 'over 70 per cent between the first and second quarters of 1975 - from $2.9 billion to $4.9 billion'. (12)

OPEC's concentration of their foreign investments within the Euro-pool could be attributed to the following reasons:

(1) They see their investment in the domestic financial markets outlets for direct investment despite the great degree of liquidity and marketability these markets offer. For these domestic markets have not yet opened up sufficiently to accept major injections of such investment and have not become adequately prepared

to accept such types of investment. The ability of foreign investors in these markets is restricted by several investment obstacles such as:

(a) The purchasing of a controlling interest in an existing company.
(b) The selling of an interest in a company.
(c) The transferring of capital into a country for direct investment.
(d) The transferring of capital out of a country in cases of disinvestment.
(e) The transferring of loan capital in and out of a country in conjunction with direct investment.
(f) The transferring of profits, royalties, interest or service fees out of a country.
(g) The exercising of control through the appointment of nominees to the management of a company, irrespective of the nationality of such nominees, and
(h) The issuing of securities in the capital market in the country of investment.

Hence as OPEC funds are not permitted into direct investment in domestic markets, that is why a high proportion goes into the Euro-markets instead.

(2) The rapid growth of Euro-markets could be also attributed to the continuous attempts by the various monetary and fiscal authorities in the US and Europe to impose regulations on foreign business in their own domestic credit markets. So we see that the imposition by some European authorities of heavy reserve requirements and negative interest rates on deposits, and so on, lead to a growing Euro-market.
(3) Coupled with Euro-markets revival was the change in the terms upon which borrowing was arranged. 'Maturities in both the Euro-bond and Euro-credit markets have shortened considerably, and the size of average loans has grown smaller in comparison to the last part of 1973 and the whole of 1974.' (13) Because of these restrictions of terms of borrowing, the Euro-market has become more attractive to the Middle Eastern investor than domestic markets.

In 1975 there occurred an upsurge of interest in Euro-bonds by oil surplus countries. The Arabs became determined to stake out a place for themselves in international finance instead of being passive suppliers of recycled money to the private banks of the West. The number of new issues in the market during 1975 doubled compared with 1974.

The oil price increase in 1973-74 made it possible for the three big Kuwaiti investment companies, the Kuwait Investment Company, the Kuwait Foreign Trading Contracting and Investment Company, and the Kuwait International Investment Company to become active on the international capital markets, making their way mostly in the underwriting and management of Euro-bond issues (both public and private).

In 1977, other Gulf-based financial institutions contributed to this international capital market. Their activities were centred on international loan syndications and lending to developing countries whether in the capacity of lead managers, managers, co-managers, or participants of a large number of bonds issued by developing countries and denominated in various international currencies. However, Middle East markets had directly contributed in managing international bond issues denominated in Arab convertible currencies. For example, between 1974 and 1979, a large number of international bond issues (private placements and public issues) had been denominated in Kuwaiti dinars, Bahraini dinars, UAE dirhams, and Saudi riyals, with the 'Kuwaiti dinar Euro-bond being the third largest sector in the entire Euro-capital market in terms of volume of new issues after the dollar and the deutschmark'. (14) Between 1974 and 1979 there were 60 international public issues of KD bonds, amounting to a total value of KD 397.5 million and 12 private placements, amounting to KD 153.5 million at the end of 1979. The principal borrowers on the KD bond market were developing countries who borrowed 31 public issues out of the 60, or 57 per cent of the funds.

As for investment in foreign domestic markets, Arab investment in the United States market is very large indeed. Such investment is divided into two types: portfolio investment and direct investment. Foreign portfolio investment refers to investment in US securities 'in voting stocks involving less than 10 per cent ownership by the foreign investor, in non-voting stocks, and in debt instruments with maturities of more than one year by persons residing in foreign countries', (15) while direct investment refers to 'the value of foreign parents' direct claims on assets of their US officiates, net of claim of these officiates on their parents' assets'. (16)

The Arab motivation for foreign portfolio investment in the US domestic market is for several reasons:

(a) long-term capital gains anticipated;
(b) the economic and political stability of the US which offers smaller risk than other countries;
(c) the large size and liquidity of US capital markets which makes possible the placement of substantial amounts of funds in a short time-span;
(d) well-organised and regulated securities markets;
(e) the wide range of investment choices;
(f) the efficient nature of US markets and availability of information;
(g) salesmanship of US brokers and dealers.

The Arab oil exporting countries emerged in 1975 as principal buyers of US securities. Their net purchase of corporate bonds amounted to $1.427 million, while their net equity investment, that is, purchases of corporate stocks, amounted to $1.441 million. (17) These capital flows were mainly due to the shift of investment of the Arab oil exporting countries from treasury bills and short-term bank certificates of deposits into longer-term assets. The Arab oil exporting countries hold third place after Europe and Canada as foreign investors in US stocks - 5.8 per cent compared with the European share of 64 per cent and the Canadian share of 13.7 per cent in 1975. (18)

So we see that foreign domestic markets are better equipped than the Euro-market to absorb larger foreign investment, since these markets have larger spread and depth. However, as these markets are subject to supervision from their local monetary and fiscal authorities, foreign investment is subject to whatever rules and regulations these institutions apply. But despite this, Arab investment in Euro-markets has been larger than those in the domestic markets: 'during 1974 and 1975 30 per cent and 27 per cent respectively of total petro-surpluses were invested in the foreign domestic markets, compared to $37\frac{1}{2}$ per cent and 45 per cent in the Euro-markets'. (19)

The involvement of Arab institutions in the Euro-markets has several reasons. First is the profitability reason, especially as 'total syndicated Euro-loans in the first half of 1977 amounted to more than $13,000 million'. (20)

Although the business is uneven in quality, any investment house with a reasonable balance sheet has the ability to take some profitable business on to its books, whether loans, underwriting or trading. The yield from Euro-bonds for an Arab house compares more favourably with domestic investment and could well be safer.

Second, the bulk of Arab funds flowing into the Euro-currency market is from direct or indirect government investment and not from the private sector. Because of their size, the Euro-markets are the only places where large sums can be invested.

Third, Arab activity in the Euro-markets give those countries the experience they need in order to make their own capital markets more efficient and better developed.

Development of the Kuwaiti dinar bond market

Bonds lead-managed by Arab banks have been almost exclusively confined to Kuwait dinar denominated issues. The reason for this was that as the financial surplus of Kuwait exceeded its local investment possibilities, it started to lend abroad on medium and long-terms. To protect the country's foreign assets from exchange risk and to diversify sources of national income away from oil production, 'the Kuwaiti institutions have more turned their attention to their own capital markets for the management of issuers'. (21) Kuwait's foreign financial investments were moved away from paper denominated in foreign currencies to instruments denominated in Kuwaiti dinars (KD), a determination on their part 'to bring the Kuwaiti market increasingly into their own rather than keep them as mere appendages of the Euro-markets'. (22)

During the period 1967-74, markets dealings were only with private placements of bonds issued by multinational financial institutions such as the World Bank. However, between 1974 and 1977 international public issues started with a size ranging from KD 3 million to KD 10 million, five years' maturities, and 15 to 30 selling members, almost entirely from Kuwait and other Arab countries. In 1978, the KD bond market witnessed a marked development when 15 issues for international borrowers totalled KD 122 million. The reasons for this development were 'an active secondary market, a high domestic liquidity, rising dollar interest rates, low short-term KD rates, and the successful introduction of certificates of deposits (CDs)'. (23) A marked increase was also noticeable in the size of issues and number of selling members - around 40-52 institutions. Of the KD bond issues in the 1970s, five were floated for Arab borrowers for the financing of specific development projects which 'points out the strong participation by Kuwait in the recycling of capital within the area on pure commercial terms'. (24)

Although the KD bond market continued to improve, it had to face structural difficulties which led to a high cost of raising capital on the KD markets and resulted in an illiquidity of KD bonds and a rigidity in the pricing of new issues, due until recently to the lack of a secondary market.

At the local level, as investors in the KD market had a limited choice between short-term bank deposits and medium and long-term bonds, they had to resort to foreign currency financial assets to satisfy their investment requirements. So, in order to attract deposits on a longer term and to lengthen the average maturity of their loans, banks in Kuwait decided to issue medium-term certificates of deposits (CDs), whose liquidity improved only after the establishment of independent secondary market-makers in 1977. Accordingly, as the CD market became more efficient, long-term CD rates fell relative to short-term rates. As a result, there occurred a lowering in the cost of raising long-term capital in Kuwait, both for local and international borrowers.

In addition to the growth in the KD bond market, there was the establishment, in April 1977, of a new company, the Arab Company for Trading Securities (ACTS), with 65 per cent of the shares held by the Kuwait International Investment Company and the other 35 per cent by the Industrial Bank of Kuwait, 'Created to promote and develop in Kuwait a viable secondary market for fixed income securities denominated in Kuwaiti dinars'. (25) As a market-maker, ACTS is maintaining an active secondary market in almost all domestic and international bonds denominated in KD, with a turnover reaching KD 150 million in its second year of operation.

Reasons for the lack of success of Arabs in the Euro-bond market

(1) Nature of the market: Euro-bond issues have remained

in the hands of a select group of securities houses. Thus mandates for Euro-bond issues have tended to be awarded to this club of houses.

(2) Lack of experience in the securities business: as Arab financial intermediaries have been confined to deposit and loan activity, thus they are orientated towards spread lending and on-balance-sheet income and have little experience in risk taking in new issues underwriting and securities trading.

(3) Arab investment banks have always been short of sufficient experience, professionalism and connections.

(4) Capability to direct securities to final takers is lacking, as Arab houses have been limiting the scope of their placement largely to their own governments or buying securities for their own accounts.

International credit makers in the 1980s, as opposed to the 1970s, are no longer able to absorb petro-surpluses. At present, the Euro-banks' absorptive capacity to borrow and take-up more loans is questionable. Therefore, the Arab countries saw the need to invest directly a major proportion of their surpluses outside the system of Euro-lending.

Since 1979, many oil producing countries have decided to direct more of their longer-term investments towards the setting up of new well-capitalised Arab banks or towards increasing the capital of existing banks. Also, new privately owned banks were created with a large capital. This wave of capital injections, estimated at $6-7 billion, has given Arab Euro-lending a sound securities base, upon which it can buy risks directly. As such, banks are without big commitments, and as liquidity in the international markets contracted over the years, their few country-limit problems and their access to OPEC liquidity will put them in a competitive position to attract deposits from all sources. In this way, Arab banks, with a more secure capital and deposit-raising, will be enabled to fill much of the gap in meeting the financial needs of the developing world, and 'will tend to take a longer-term view of profitability and will be prepared in the short run to write loans at aggressive margins with a view to developing international asset growth strategies rather than concentrating on immediate profitability'. (26)

Arab banks' underwriting of bond issues when compared to their exposure in the Euro-loan market has been very limited; exclusively confined to Kuwait dinar-denominated issues. Therefore, extending Arab involvement in the international bond market is very important, as the Euro-credits are witnessing a slow-down: 'in 1983 the value of total Euro-credits completed amounted to $73.9 billion, down from $133.4 billion in 1981', (27) in contrast to the rapid stepping-up in international bond finance, 'the value of international bonds issued in 1983 amounted to $75.8 billion, up from $52.9 billion in 1981'. (28)

IV LIKELY PROSPECTS FOR INCREASED LINKAGES BETWEEN DIFFERENT ARAB DOMESTIC MARKETS

As the problems in the Arab region relate to the question of harmonising the long-term investment interests of the oil producing countries with the financial needs for development and investment purposes of other developing countries in the region, the establishment of Arab financial intermediaries is very important. This will facilitate the transfer of private and public capital within the region through its own financial markets. In recent years, the surplus Arab countries have directed a large part of their financial resources to capital-needy Arab countries, reflected in increasing official grants and lending to finance development projects and to relieve foreign exchange difficulties. On the other hand, private capital flow remained rather small due to institutional obstacles in many countries.

Borrowing by Arab countries on the international bond market, in the form of public issues and private placements, constituted about $1.5 billion during 1972-78. During that same period, the volume of borrowing by Arab countries on Euro-currency credit markets amounted to $14.5 billion, excluding unpublicised credits. Despite the deficiency in Arab financial intermediation, some progress has been observed due to efforts taken at both the official and private levels.

'The focus on Arab capital markets by businessmen and politicians has been encouraged by the structural contractions in the Arab regions that were magnified by the oil price increases of the 1970s and the appearance of the so-called oil financial surpluses.' (29) As capital-abundant Arab countries are accumulating liquid assets in excess of their present ability to absorb capital, and the deficit Arab countries are suffering from a lack of capital, a harmonisation of the long-term investment interests of the

121

surplus countries with the development needs and economic potentials of the deficit countries is needed. To do this, the development of an Arab capital market is necessary.

Arab capital markets suffer from shortcomings due to an imbalance between the supply and demand for capital at different maturity levels. The markets also suffer from smallness of size and high liquidity preference by investors whereas 'the demand for funds is of a longer-term nature and sometimes needs a concessional component due to the low internal rate of return on the average project'. (30) Here, a question concerning the prospect of integrating Arab capital markets arises in consideration of the possible disparities in the saving rates between different countries, and in the type of institutions needed to transform short money into long money and to effect transfer of capital between high and low-saving areas.

During the past few years, monetary and fiscal authorities of many Arab countries have taken important measures to strengthen Arab financial co-operation. These include:

(a) Measures aimed at developing local capital markets: such measures concerned themselves primarily with improving the efficiency of local institutions, instruments and legislation with respect to debt and equity markets. The degrees of specialisation of each local Arab market will depend on several factors such as 'the availability of resources, the degree of openness to other countries of the region, the communications network and the amount of private initiative. For example, the Kuwaiti dinar Euro-bond market has grown to a total float of $2 billion.' (31) As a result of this growth, some Arab borrowers had easier access to Kuwaiti markets. The same could be said of the Amman markets whose development has led to the involvement of more Arab money in the financing of Jordanian projects.

(b) Bilateral financial co-operation: this has involved measures which support development funds or banks, such as the Kuwait Fund for Economic Development, the Saudi Development Fund, the Libyan Arab Foreign Bank, the Abu Dhabi Fund for Economic Development and the Iraqi External Fund. Also included are government-to-government loans. However, financial operations of this kind 'are usually conducted outside the market mechanism and as such are termed off-market transactions'. (32)

(c) Multilateral financial co-operation: two major multilateral Arab institutions have been created, the Arab Monetary Fund and the Arab Fund for Economic and Social Development. Other important institutions are the Inter-Arab Investment Guarantee Corporation, and the Unified Arab Investment Agreement, which was signed in November 1980 at the Arab Economic Summit in Amman. In addition, other multilateral institutions have been established in different specialised sectors, such as the Arab Petroleum Investment Corporation sponsored by the Organisation of Arab Petroleum Exporting Countries, the Arab Maritime Transport Company, the Arab Mining Company and the Arab Company for Livestock Development.

Efforts at the private level have consisted of an increasing regional flow of funds through existing and newly founded Arab financial institutions, including:

(a) Private equity financing which varied from real estate agreements to the creation of many joint Arab Companies. The interest in this form of private financing is shared both by the host countries and the capital exporting countries. 'The capital-importing countries are relieved from additional costs of debt servicing - this is particularly important for Arab countries which are heavily indebted and have approached their borrowing limits; the surplus countries participate in the productive facilities of the region and are not merely money-lenders.' (33) As this form of investment is restricted by the industrial countries, equity investment flows among Arab countries should be increased. The most important expression of this form of investment is joint ventures as they 'contribute to the expansion of the absorptive capacity of Arab countries in order to enable them to accommodate large injections of surplus funds'. (34)

(b) Lending activities: Arab financial institutions have increased their participation in international lending and in Euro-currency loans to Arab borrowers as well as in bond issues, such as the development of one advanced sector in the international bond market denominated in an Arab currency, namely, the Kuwait dinar international bond market. 'Of the Kuwait dinar bond issues floated on the market, over 40 per cent were for Arab borrowers and for project financing in the Arab world.' (35) Recently, there was an increase in private flows among Arab countries in the form of debt financing. The specialisation of different local markets and their effects on other Arab countries has varied: 'Kuwait has emerged as a capital exporter in the Arab world (in-to-out-market); and Amman has developed a financial market to attract Arab capital for local use (out-to-in-market)'. (36) These centres represent different models of capital flow within the Arab region which would provide a starting basis for recycling Arab financial surpluses within the region.

(c) Mixed (official/private) regional financing: capital markets in many Arab countries contain many shortcomings which are not due to a lack of overall savings, but rather to an imbalance between the supply and demand for capital at different maturity levels. The investors' liquidity preference within undeveloped and small markets is very high, whereas they demand funds of a longer-term nature which sometimes need a concessional component due to the low interest rate of return on the average project. Thus, the prospect of integrating Arab capital markets poses the question of the possible differences in the savings rates between different countries, and in the types of new institutions needed to transform short money into long money and so to effect transfer of capital between high and low-saving areas. The composition of the available funds reflects the way in which financing requirements are met, and although the supply of long-term money in the aid sector is extensive, most funds, including government funds, are short-term deposits. Thus, this transformation needs the setting up of Euro-banking groups based abroad and in the Arab world.

The establishment of an integrated Arab market is needed because of the grouping size of the funds available, which is facilitated by offering Arab ventures more opportunities of obtaining non-local sources of capital that can help them expand to the size needed for efficient operation on a regional scale: bringing the conditions on which finance can be obtained in different Arab markets more in line with each other and so reducing the present distortions; increasing the capital supply as financial savings are attracted to the market by the wider range of investment outlets; intensifying financial flows and reducing the risk of disturbance that is characteristic of excessively narrow markets.

The difficulty here lies in assessing the actual degree of integration among the Arab capital markets. These are large linkages with international capital markets when compared to those between markets themselves. The weak integration of Arab capital markets is indicated by the large volume of borrowing and investent which the Arab entities undertook through the Euro-markets. For example, it is shown that the volume of Arab borrowing in the Euro-bond market and in the Euro-currency markets during the period 1972-84, in the form of public issues and private placements, was $2.5 billion and $43.5 billion respectively. (37) These borrowings took the form of floating rate syndicated bank credits which were completed to finance specific projects, balance of payments deficits and budgetary deficits. Therefore, the volume of total Arab borrowing (banks and credits) is around $46 billion.

Between 1972 and 1984, the Euro-markets did not only accommodate the main investment outlet for the financial surpluses generated and accumulated by the Arab region. The fact was, Arab investment in the Euro-markets was huge and exceeded the demand for loans in the region. Therefore, as there exists a large gap in Arab intermediation, to achieve a better degree of financial equilibrium in the region necessitates bridging this gap. The challenge to developing an Arab capital market lies in 'transferring the region's potential demand for loanable funds into an effective or real demand - or to use the investment bankers' jargon - "bankable demand" - while simultaneously reaping the benefits derived from investment outside the region', (38) which, in short, means providing the real balance between local, regional and international investment.

Arab financial integration requires the correct management of individual domestic markets. Deficit Arab countries have to manage their economies in such a way that scarcity of capital is adequately reflected in the cost of funds without imposing ceilings on interest rates: such ceilings lead to a low growth in financial savings and eventual misallocation of resources. Therefore, the right capital price would force resources to move into the highest yielding projects. In deficit Arab countries, the government should finance itself through more taxes and issues of securities at market price so as to create the right environment for capital accumulation. On the other hand, surplus Arab countries should manage their economies in such a way that the abundance of capital is reflected in lower financial returns, whereas at present, overseas financial investment keeps domestic interest rates up. Financial assets should be priced in relation to real economic development thereby reducing misallocations of capital.

From the above discussion, it becomes obvious that direct integration as the means of achieving free-flow of capital between Arab countries is not present at the moment. What has been occurring up to now has been indirect integration via Arab Euro-banking. Between 1976 and 1984, Arab banks' participation as lead managers in the Euro-loan market has totalled $36.4 billion. Of these, $16.2 billion were Euro-loans managed for Arab borrowers. In 1983, 51 per cent of total Arab lending Euro-loans were for Arab borrowers, while in 1984 it grew to 54 per cent or $700 million.

V   OBSTACLES TO THE STRENGTHENING OF INTER-MARKET RELATIONSHIPS

The obstacles to a strengthening of relationships among the capital markets in the Arab world are similar to those that hamper the growth of capital markets at national levels; economic, institutional and legal.

The stage of economic development of most Arab countries does not, as yet, provide the necessary basis for a significant network of equity capital flow within the region. These countries do not possess financial institutions, markets for assets and investment partners of comparable quality, efficiency or size. They lack the secondary markets and specialised investment and issuing houses. Nevertheless, in the semi-industrialised countries of the region, the size of a number of local enterprises and their managerial capacity are already adequate for them to make direct investments within the area, if institutional and legal factors are favourable.

The following statement on monetary stability, made in connection with the European Economic Community, holds true for the Arab region. 'The progress made in establishing an integrated capital market will depend first and foremost on the general stability of currencies and on the extent to which public finances are correctly managed.' (39) In fact, several years of currency stability preceded the signing of the Treaty of Rome, and this, along with eliminating all restrictions on current payments among member countries, has been a major factor in the growth of trade within the community. Monetary stability, increasing trade flows and stability-increasing trade flows, and the loosening of most restriction on capital movements have strengthened the links among the members' capital markets.

As such, the great differences in exchange rate stability among the various Arab countries inhibits movement of equity capital to countries with unstable currencies because of the exchange risk involved. The disadvantages of monetary instability for the investor are offset only in part by the higher nominal yields that such countries offer. For 'to undertake an obligation in a foreign currency brings with it an element of uncertainty as to the final cost of the operation'. (40)

Other problems include the following:

(1) Investors with preference for a fairly liquid placement do not choose to invest in the Arab region because of its undiversified and unestablished banking system.
(2) Where the preference is for marketable assets, the range of investment opportunities in shares, equities, real estate and other forms of investment available are fairly small, and the markets in which these assets can be bought or sold easily and efficiently are not well enough developed in the Arab regions to make investment in these countries attractive.
(3) In the case of direct investment in new ventures, these countries will hardly appeal to the investor because of the unavailability of potential partners, with technological, financial or commercial resources.
(4) Availability of information about good investment outlets in Arab countries is minimal.

As for the institutional and legal framework within which the Arab capital markets operate, it is not conducive to the strengthening of their mutual links. This is because the national structures channel local capital as much as possible toward domestic investment. At the same time, local capital authorised to move abroad goes outside the region.

Arab countries permit the purchase of foreign securities by residents but prohibit the sale of domestic securities to non-residents, except in Jordan and Kuwait under specific provisions. Investors in securities of other member countries listed on a stock exchange of the country of issue should be encouraged.

Another institutional obstacle to an increase in capital movements within the Arab region results from the diversity of taxes and tax rates on corporate profits, dividends and interest, as well as on security transactions in addition to the great variety of tax exemptions.

Other obstacles include the following:

(1) Investment instruments directed to the public are few in the region. In the case of availability of public issues of securities, they are usually restricted to nationals of the country of issue, or they are small denomination and aggregate size.

(2) Linkages between organized institutions of the established financial centres are non-existent. For example, the equity securities traded in Beirut or Kuwait do not have access to the securities markets in any other country of the region.

(3) Officials and administrators of countries of the region do not understand the legal aspects of financial transactions. Issuers of financial instruments and investors in these financial instruments and assets are in doubt as to whether the transfer of title, ownership rights, inheritance rights, taxability, and mobility, in a regional context, maintain the original legal contractual arrangements of the securities in question.

In the absence of these restrictions there would be investment opportunities with high returns because 'an Arab investment in an Arab country yields a direct return to the Arab investor as well as an indirect benefit arising from the contribution to the economic development of the Arab country in which the funds are invested and the Arab country investing the fund'. (41)

NOTES

1. Imady, M. (1982) 'The role of Arab development funds', The Arab Gulf Journal, vol. 2, no. 2, October.
2. Nashashibi, H. (1979) Arab development ... through co-operation and financial markets, Kuwait: Al-Shaya Publishing House, p. 47.
3. Harik, A. (1984) 'Financial integration in the Arab East: problems and prospects' in Guecioueur, A., The problems of Arab economic development and integration,

(ed.), Colorado: Westview Press Inc. p. 83.

4.   Nashashibi, H. (1980) 'Financial resources for development; capital markets in developing countries: a study on borrowing by developing countries in the emerging capital markets of the Middle East', OAPEC Bulletin, vol. 6, no. 10, October.

5.   Harik, A. (1984) 'Financial integration in the Arab East: problems and prospects' in Guecioueur, A., The problems of Arab economic development and integration, (ed.), Colorado: Westview Press Inc., p. 85.

6.   Ibid. p. 88.

7.   Ibid. pp. 88-9.

8.   Ibid. p. 89.

9.   Nashashibi, H. (1980) 'Financial resources for development; capital markets in developing countries: a study on borrowing by developing countries in the emerging capital markets of the Middle East', OAPEC Bulletin, vol. 6, no. 10, October.

10.   Nashashibi, H. (1980) 'Major developments in the Arab financial intermediation', OAPEC Bulletin, vol. 6, no. 1, January.

11.   Nashashibi, H. (1979) Arab development ... through co-operation and financial markets, Kuwait: Al-Shaya Publishing House, p. 21.

12.   Ibid. p. 21.

13.   Ibid. pp. 22-3.

14.   Nashashibi, H. (1980) 'Financial resources for development; capital markets in developing countries: a study on borrowing by developing countries in the emerging capital markets of the Middle East', OAPEC Bulletin, vol. 6, no. 10, October.

15.   El Mallakh, R., Kadhim, M. and Paulson, B. (1977) Capital investment in the Middle East, USA: Praeger Publishers, p. 170.

16.   Ibid. p. 170.

17.   Ibid. p. 172.

18.   Ibid. p. 174.

19.   Nashashibi, H. (1979) Arab development ... through co-operation and financial markets, Kuwait: Al-Shaya Publishing House, p. 35.

20.   'Activity of OPEC lenders points to eventual inter-Arab market' (1977) Middle East Economic Digest, Special Report, December.

21.   Field, P. (1980) 'Euromarkets: their role in Middle East finance', Middle East Annual Review.

22.   Nashashibi, H, Kasseim, O. (1974) 'Bringing Kuwait's financial market up to date', Euromoney, August.

23.   Nashashibi, H. (1980) 'Financial resources for development; capital markets in developing countries: a study on borrowing by developing countries in the emerging capital markets of the Middle East', OAPEC Bulletin, vol. 6, no. 10, October.

24.   Nashashibi, H. (1979) Arab development ... through co-operation and financial markets, Kuwait: Al-Shaya Publishing House, p. 63.

25.   Nashashibi, H. (1980) 'Financial resources for development; capital markets in developing countries: a study on borrowing by developing countries in the emerging capital markets of the Middle East', OAPEC Bulletin, vol. 6, no. 10, October.

26.   Nashashibi, H. (1985) 'Arab to Arab Euro-bonds can work', Euromoney, May.

27.   Nashashibi, H. (1984) 'Challenges confronting Arab banking and Arab capital markets', The Arab Gulf Journal, vol. 4, no. 2, October.

28.   Ibid.

29.   Ibid.

30.   Ibid.

31.   Nashashibi, H. (1982) 'The development and integration of Arab capital markets', OAPEC Bulletin, vol. 8, no. 11, November.

32.   Nashashibi, H. (1980) 'Financial resources for development of capital markets in developing countries: a study on borrowing by developing countries in the emerging capital markets of the Middle East', paper presented at a conference on 'Trade and Development', organised by the United Nations, Geneva, 3 July.

33.   Ibid.

34.   Ibid.

35.   Nashashibi, H. (1979) Arab development ... through co-operation and financial markets, Kuwait: Al-Shaya Publishing House p. 60.

36.   Nashashibi, H. (1981) 'The changing role of Arab capital markets', Dinar, vol. 1, no. 2.

37.   Nashashibi, H. (1984) 'Challenges confronting Arab banking and capital markets', The Arab Gulf Journal, vol. 4, no. 2, October.

38.   Ibid.

39.   Commission of the EEC (1966) The development of a European capital market, report by a group of experts

under the direction of C. Segre, Brussels, November, p. 14.

40. Segre, C. (1963) 'Financial markets in the EEC: prospects for integration', <u>Moorgate and Wall Street</u>, August.

41. 'Inter-Arab co-operation - migration and investment' (1986) <u>OAPEC Bulletin</u>, vol. 12, no. 6, June.

CONCLUSIONS AND FUTURE RECOMMENDATIONS

The measures that will be required in the long run to strengthen the relationships between the capital markets of the Arab countries will be briefly outlined here. These measures could be the beginning of a cycle leading to the creation of widespread integration and the eventual free-movement of goods, services, persons and capital among the member countries.

The first task is to make the various national markets more effective. Efforts should be made by these countries to eliminate the numerous obstacles which restrict or distort the flow of savings to various intermediaries and then to investors.

It could be assumed that with monetary stability, the exchange-rate systems in the area will be co-ordinated and that freedom of payments on current account will be generally applied. Those countries which will maintain controls on capital accounts could, probably, make a distinction between transactions with other countries of the Arab region and those with the rest of the world.

Another major area of reform is the numerous legal and administrative provisions pertaining to the financial institutions, which have created a series of separate circuits of capital funds within each country. This poses the question to what extent special incentives are to be offered for the collection of savings for specific purposes so that they become available to borrowers at concessionary terms. The issue has wide branches stemming from national development policies and methods of implementation. Nevertheless, the possibility of capital market integration will be substantially prevented unless common changes are made in this field.

From an institutional standpoint, in so far as commercial banks engage in foreign activities, these consist almost entirely of short-term financing of traditional exports. Eventually, a stronger need will be felt for standardising commercial banking practices. At the same time, the growing number of branches established by banks of various Arab countries elsewhere in the region will assume an increased importance in the financial aspects of regional integration.

Up to now, significant measures to encourage the participation of the various financial institutions in the other capital markets in the region have not been adopted. For example, a few years ago the Arab League embarked upon a plan for the creation of an Arab Union of Stock Exchanges which would promote co-operation between the existing markets and any new ones that might develop within the Arab world, and would endeavour to set common standards and procedures for their operation. The initiative has been lost in the aftermath of the isolation of Egypt following Camp David. This participation could be attained if such institutions (commercial banks, savings banks, investment banks, mutual funds, insurance companies) were authorised to invest just a fraction of their resources in securities issued in other Arab countries. A significant role could also be played by the development banks in the region, whose co-operation is important, particularly for the financing of projects affecting two or more countries. Co-operation of this kind could take various forms, such as equity investment in different enterprises or the underwriting of bonds floated in the respective countries.

As discussed previously, the registration of securities of other Arab countries is either non-existent or negligible on the stock exchanges of the region. Nevertheless, as has become apparent at the various meetings of representatives of stock exchanges which were held in Jordan in 1983 and Tunisia in 1984, (1) there is a growing awareness of the need to develop inter-regional trading in securities. As such, the Union of the stock exchanges formulated a number of recommendations aiming, among other things, to standardise various types of operations and practices. These concern the financial information that listed corporations should submit periodically to the exchanges, particularly their balance sheets and profit and loss statements. Another set of recommendations is intended to give greater protection to investors mainly by requiring the issuing corporations to make public any major changes in their organisation, assets, or prospects.

Although such action will be encouraged by the Union, a significant growth in the regional trade of Arab securities depends mainly on the improvement of certain economic conditions, particularly a greater stability of the currencies, the strengthening of the securities' markets at the national level and freedom of payments.

POSSIBLE ROLE OF THE REGIONAL FINANCIAL INSTITUTIONS

The process of capital market integration is a result of the functional behaviour of the intermediary role of many regional financial institutions. Until now, the regional financial institutions have had mainly an indirect role in the strengthening of the capital markets in the Arab world and in bringing about closer links between them. A regional financial institution such as the Arab Monetary Fund (AMF) has given considerable attention over the past few years to the issue of capital market integration. The Fund participated with other regional organisations, such as the Union of Arab Stock Exchanges, in conducting a survey of domestic capital markets in the Arab world. A group of experts found that the main shortcomings were related to the inadequate diversification of the investment instruments available to these markets, the lack of secondary markets and of specialised investment and issuing houses, the lack of suitable domestic financial legislation and the almost complete absence of linkages among the domestic capital markets in the Arab countries. In the light of these findings, the Fund has adopted an operational plan based on: (2)

(1) direct intervention in the domestic markets, aimed at promoting their development through technical assistance, and participation in the establishment of appropriate secondary markets and issuing institutions;

(2) identifying and implementing the measures needed to foster stronger links among domestic markets, through relaxation and eventual abolition of existing restrictions on the re-registration and negotiation, in one Arab country, of financial papers originating in the capital markets of another;

(3) more active intervention by the AMF and other Arab regional financial institutions to foster the growth of a market in securities, by issuing marketable securities in its own name or on behalf of its members and by adopting appropriate measures to ensure an active secondary market in these securities.

Another task of the AMF was their participation in the drafting of an investment agreement which would provide adequate guarantees for across-the-border investments against non-commercial risks, and define a minimum standard for tax exemptions and other incentives aimed at promoting a greater flow of capital between Arab countries. Although the agreement has been approved by the Economic and Social Council of the League of Arab States, it still awaits ratification by member countries.

Regional institutions could make a more direct contribution to the stimulation of local capital markets by requiring the borrower, in the case of loans to private corporations, to offer a significant proportion of his shares to the general public over a period of time. These institutions must also subscribe part of the capital of development finance companies so that other investors, domestic and foreign, take part in the venture. In time, such finance companies can contribute to the development of a capital market by selling from their portfolios, securities of concerns, or, by underwriting share issues of enterprises they are promoting.

Another method to be used by the regional financial institutions to strengthen local capital markets would be the creation of a multinational subsidiary whose functions would include guaranteeing certain bond issues or other obligations, denominated in one or more local currencies and publicly issued in one or more of the member countries, against the risk of default and non-transferability. To find acceptance, such bonds would have to carry a realistic rate of interest in terms of the prevailing conditions in the markets concerned. The resources of such a subsidiary need not be very large, provided that they are adequate in view of the risks involved. Some countries would have to consider the question of whether an external guarantee should be given to domestic bond issues as they can, under certain circumstances, be a useful means of stemming the outflow of local private capital and directing it into productive investment.

Another recommendation that will contribute to integration of the capital markets of the region would be the 'creation of a market-making financial institution for regional risk-taking, similar to the market-making functions of ACTS in the Kuwait market'. (3) Its role would include the risk taking in the marketing of securities issued for the financing of regional development projects or those issued by business enterprises operating on a regional basis. Public and private funds, development banks and organisations should have access to these securities on a subscription basis. The immediate liquidity of all portfolio securities marketed by this regional market-maker should be provided to show the liquid nature of the securities being subscribed.

In addition, organising such a regional market-maker requires substantial commitment of capital and expertise on the part of the various funds and development and commercial banks. Although capitalisation is not a problem to the Arab region, the expertise poses problems given the region's shortage of trained and experienced professionals in financial services.

The establishment of such a regional market-making organisation would change the role played by the established financial institutions of the region from intermediating in liquidity-oriented investment and asset management to encouraging financial institutions in their ability to secure a market-making environment. The portfolio of financial institutions' financial assets would help release substantial funds, currently held in liquid form or placed on international financial markets, to the regional equity market.

In conclusion, the establishment of a regional market-making framework must include several areas of concern. One of these is to determine how issuers of securities on the local level can benefit from regional marketing and distribution by the market-maker. Another is the ability of the market-maker to enter the local financial market in search of interested individual investors. It is important for the local financial institutions to adjust their legal and financial structures so as not to conflict with the day-to-day operations of the market-maker.

One effect of market integration to be obtained by the removal of existing barriers and by giving greater freedom of action to institutional investors, would be to ensure greater stability of issue conditions and price movements. Another effect would be to give the community the character of a financial centre vis-à-vis other countries. This would offer the investor a variety of investment possibilities, thus encouraging a closer interest in the markets for public and private securities. It is hoped that this would stop the frequent tendency to channel too many resources into the purchase of real estate and luxury goods.

NOTES

1.   Arab Monetary Fund (1983) <u>Annual Report, 1983, 1984</u>.
2.   Arab Monetary Fund (1984) <u>Annual Report, 1982, 1983 and 1984</u>.
3.   Harik, A. (1984) 'Financial integration in the Arab East: problems and prospects' in Guecioueur, A., <u>The problems of Arab economic development and integration</u>, (ed.) Colorado, Westview Press Inc., p. 93.

BIBLIOGRAPHY

A. BOOKS

1. Abdeen, A. and Shook, D. The Saudi financial system, New York: John Wiley and Sons, 1984.
2. Achilli, M. and Khaldi, M. The role of the Arab development funds in the world economy, London: Croom Helm, 1984.
3. Agtmael, A. Emerging securities market, London: Euromoney Publications, 1984.
4. Ali, T. Economic integration as a strategy for economic development: prospects for five Arab gulf states, un-published Dissertation, University of Colorado at Boulder, 1980.
5. Aliboni, R. Arab industrialisation and economic integration, London: Croom Helm, 1979.
6. Andic, F., Andic, S. and Dosser, D. A theory of economic integration for development countries, London: George Allen and Unwin, 1971.
7. Bain, A. The economics of the financial system, Oxford: Martin Robertson, 1981.
8. Balassa, B. (ed.) European economic integration, New York: American Elsevier Publishing Company Inc., 1975.
9. Balassa, B. The theory of economic integration, London: George Allen and Unwin, 1962.
10. Basch, A. and Kybal, M. Capital markets in Latin America, London: Praeger Publishers, 1970.
11. Basch, A. Capital markets of the European economic community: problems of integration, Michigan: The University of Michigan Press, 1965.

12.   Bertoneche, M. European securities markets: efficiency, international diversification and prospects of integration, Michigan: Ann Arbor, 1978.

13.   Bicksler, J. (ed.) Capital market equilibrium and efficiency, Toronto: D.C. Heath and Company, 1977.

14.   Bracewell-Milnes, P. Economic integration in east and west, London: Croom Helm, 1976.

15.   Brealey, R. and Myers, S. Principles of corporate finance, London: McGraw-Hill, 1984.

16.   Calamanti, A. The securities market and under-development, Milan: Giuffre Publisher, 1983.

17.   Cooper, C. and Alexander, S. Economic development and population growth in the Middle East, New York: American Elsevier Publishing Company, 1972.

18.   Copeland, T. Financial theory and corporate policy, London: Addison-Wesley Publishing Company, 1983.

19.   Corden, W. Monetary integration: essays in international finance, no. 93, New Jersey: Princeton University, 1972.

20.   Demir, S. Arab development funds in the Middle East, USA: Pergamon Press, 1979.

21.   Djavadi, D. Economic integration in the Middle East, unpublished dissertation, Claremont Graduate School, 1977.

22.   Edens, D. Oil and development in the Middle East, USA: Praeger Publishers, 1979.

23.   EL-Agraa, A. International economic integration, London: Macmillan Press, 1982.

24.   EL-Azhary, M. The impact of oil revenues on Arab gulf development, London: Croom Helm, 1984.

25.   EL-Beblawi, H. and Fahmi, R. The Kuwait stock market (1946-1980), no. 6, Kuwait: the Industrial Bank of Kuwait, 1982.

26.   EL-Mallakh, R. Economic development and regional co-operation: Kuwait, Chicago: the University of Chicago Press, 1968.

27.   EL-Mallakh, R., Kadhim, M. and Paulson, B. Capital investment in the Middle East, USA: Praeger Publishers, 1977.

28.   Field, P. and Moore, A. (eds) Arab financial market, London: Euromoney Publications, 1981.

29.   Ghantus, E. Arab industrial integration, London: Croom Helm, 1982.

30.   Gorostiaga, X. The role of the international financial centres in underdeveloped countries, London:

Croom Helm, 1984.

31.   Guecioueur, A. The problems of Arab economic development and integration, Colorado: Westview Press Inc., 1984.

32.   Hanson, J. A dictionary of economics and commerce, London: Macdonald and Evans, 1977.

33.   Harik, E. Economic integration in less developed countries: prospects for six Arab countries, unpublished dissertation, Wayne State University, 1978.

34.   Haseeb, K. and Makdisi, S. (eds) Arab monetary integration, London: Croom Helm, 1980.

35.   Hatem, S. The possibilities of economic co-operation and integration between the European and the Arab league, Munchen: Florentz, 1981.

36.   Hawawini, G. and Michel, P. (eds) European equity markets: risk return and efficiency, New York: Garland Publishing Inc., 1984.

37.   Kindleberger, C. The formation of financial centres, New Jersey: Princeton University Press, 1974.

38.   Lees, F. and Eng, M. International financial markets, New York: Praeger Publishers, 1975.

39.   Machlup, F. (ed.) Economic integration worldwide, regional, sectoral, New York: Macmillan Press, 1976.

40.   Machlup, F. A history of thought on economic integration, New York: Macmillan Press, 1977.

41.   Makdisi, S. Financial policy and economic growth, New York: Columbia University Press, 1979.

42.   Merse, F. AL-Tamwel Al-Masre fi litanmia Al Eqlesadia, Al-Eskandria: Al-Marif Al-Eskandria, 1980.

43.   Morgan, E. and Harrington, R. Capital markets in the EEC, London: Wilton House Publications, 1977.

44.   Myrdal, G. An international economy, New York: Harper and Row, 1956.

45.   Nashashibi, H. Arab development ... through co-operation and financial markets, Kuwait: Alshaya Publishing House, 1979.

46.   Nugent, J. and Thomas, T. Bahrain and the Gulf, London: Croom Helm, 1985.

47.   Rose, H. The economic background to investment, Cambridge: the Syndics of the Cambridge University Press, 1960.

48.   Saunders, C. (ed.) Regional integration in East and West, London: Macmillan Press, 1983.

49.   Sayegh, K. Oil and Arab regional development, USA: Greenwood Press Publishers, 1978.

50. Sayigh, Y. The Arab economy, New York, Oxford University Press, 1982.

51. Schmidt, H. Advantages and disadvantages of an integrated market compared with a fragmented market, Brussels: Commission of the European Communities, 1977.

52. Sharpe, W. Investments, New Jersey: Prentice-Hall Inc., 1978.

53. Simmons, A. Arab foreign aid, London: Associated University Press, Inc., 1981.

54. Solnik, B. European capital markets, Canada: D.C. Heath & Company, 1973.

55. Underwood, A. Inter Arab financial flows, Durham: Centre of Middle Eastern and Islamic Studies, University of Durham, 1974.

56. Vajdo, I. (ed.) Integration, economic union and national state, in foreign trade in a planned economy, Cambridge: Cambridge University Press, 1971.

57. Williams, R. and Johnson, G. International capital markets: developments and prospects, Washington, D.C.: International Monetary Fund, 1982.

58. Wilson, R. Recent financial trends in the Gulf, Durham: Centre for Middle Eastern and Islamic Studies, University of Durham, 1981.

59. Wilson, R. Banking and finance in the Arab middle east, London: Macmillan Publishers, 1983.

60. Wionczek, M. (ed.) Latin American economic integration, New York: Praeger Publishers, 1966.

B. OFFICIAL PUBLICATIONS

1. Amman Financial Market, Profitability study of the companies listed at the Amman financial market (1978-1983), 1984.

2. Amman Financial Market, Statistical Review (1978-1984), (in Arabic), 1985.

3. Amman Financial Market, The Sixth Annual Report, 1983.

4. Amman Financial Market, The Seventh Annual Report, 1984.

5. Arab Monetary Fund, Annual Report, various issues.

6. Arab-Swiss Chamber of Commerce and Industry, Annual Directory, various issues.

7. Association of Banks in the Lebanon, Annual

Report, 1972.

8. Egypt Central Bank, Annual Report, various issues.

9. Egypt Central Bank, Economic Review, various issues.

10. Egypt National Bank, Economic Bulletin, various issues.

11. Industrial Development Banks, Fourteenth Annual Report and Balance Sheet, Jordan, 1978.

12. Jordan Central Bank, Annual Report, various issues.

13. Jordan Government, Amman Financial Market Law, 1976.

14. Kuwait Central Bank, Economic Report, various issues.

15. Kuwait Central Bank, Quarterly Statistical Bulletin, various issues.

16. Kuwait Central Bank, Economic Chart Book, various issues.

17. Ministry of Finance and Economy, Amiri decrees and by-laws organising Kuwait stock exchange, 11 March, 1985.

18. Ministry of Information, Investment climate and opportunities, Jordan, 1978.

19. Ministry of Information, Banking and finance in Jordan, 1979.

20. United Nations Economic Commission for Western Asia, Survey of Economic and Social Development in the ECWA Region, various issues.

21. United Nations Economic Commission for Western Asia, Studies on development problems in countries of Western Asia, 1981.

C. ARTICLES

1. 'Activity of OPEC lenders points to eventual inter-Arab market', Middle East Economic Digest, Special Report, December 1977, pp. 23-5.

2. Ali, T. 'Integration among the Arab states in the Gulf', Dinar, vol. 1, no. 5, 1984, pp. 6-8.

3. Aliber, R. 'The integration of national financial markets: a review of theory and findings', University of Chicago, pp. 1-44.

4. 'The Amman financial market', Middle East

Economic Digest, Special Report, 1983, pp. 121-2.

5.   'Arab equity', Arab Banking and Finance, vol. 2, no. 8, October 1983, pp. 13-16.

6.   'The Arabs breed a new capital market', Business Week, 18 April, 1977, p. 76.

7.   'Bahrain: local stock market stagnates', Mid East Markets, vol. 11, issue 10, 14 May, 1984, p. 8.

8.   Balassa, B. 'Towards a theory of economic integration', Kyklos, vol. 14, no. 3, 1961, pp. 1-17.

9.   Baz, F. 'Bourse', Ecochiffres, 1982, pp. 63-6.

10.   Baz, F. 'Bourse et matieres premieres', Ecochiffres, 1983, pp. 121-3.

11.   Baz, F. 'Bourse', Ecochiffres, 1984, pp. 104-8.

12.   'Beirut stock exchange re-opens', IKE, Arab Microfiche Institution, 7 September, 1977.

13.   Bertrand, R. 'Prospects for integration of European capital markets', Journal of Money, Credit, Banking, August 1969, pp. 347-9.

14.   Biger, N. 'Capital market integration - some evidence from foreign-controlled securities', Journal of Economics and Business, vol. 34, no. 3, 6 June, 1986, pp. 207-13.

15.   Bletsas, A. and Tebbutt, S. 'Thin capital markets: a case study of the Kuwaiti stock markets: a note', Applied Economics, vol. 15, no. 1, 1983, pp. 121-2.

16.   'Bright future for securities business', Mid East Markets, Arab Microfiche Institution, 14 January, 1980.

17.   'The capital market in Egypt', Investment Review, vol. 4, no. 1, April 1983, pp. 6-8.

18.   Dalmoak, M. 'Stock market: boost from privatisation', The Banker, April 1985, p. 49.

19.   Damm, W. 'The obstacles to regional integration of capital markets', Journal of Money, Credit, Banking, August 1969, pp. 328-31.

20.   'Egypt gains window into capital markets', Banker, vol. CCXXIV, no. 1648, July 1981, pp. 34-6.

21.   'Expatriates boost stock exchange', Middle East Economic Digest, vol. 123, no. 23, 18 June, 1979, p. 35.

22.   Feustel, S. 'After the bubble burst', Institutional Investor International Edition, February 1983, pp. 143-6.

23.   Field, P. 'Euromarkets - their role in Middle East finance', Middle East Annual Review, 1980, pp. 149-52.

24.   'First bourse opens: trading said slow', The Middle East Report, Arab Microfiche Institution, 5 January, 1978.

25.   'Foreign bankers urge development of capital

markets in the Gulf', An-Nahar Arab Report and Memo, vol. 8, no. 13, 14 May, 1984, pp. 9-10.

26.   Gandhi, D., Saunders, A. and Woodward, R. 'Thin capital markets: a case study of the Kuwaiti stock market', Applied Economics, vol. 12, no. 3, 1980, pp. 341-9.

27.   Gandhi, D., Saunders, A. and Woodward, R. 'Thin capital markets: a study of the Kuwaiti stock market, a reply', Applied Economics, vol. 15, no. 1, 1983, pp. 123-4.

28.   Good, D. 'Financial integration in the late nineteenth century: Austria', Journal of Economic History, vol. XXXVii, no. 4, December 1977, pp. 890-911.

29.   'Government bonds listed on stock exchange', Middle East Economic Digest, vol. 23, no. 1, 6 January, 1979, p. 22.

30.   Hawkins, B. 'Towards a European capital market', Rev. Société D'Etudes et D'Expansion, vol. 72, no. 25, 4 January, 1973, pp. 81-5.

31.   Hessels, J. 'Prospects and problems of an integrated European securities market', Euromoney, March 1973, pp. 4-8.

32.   Hoyle, M. 'Monetary integration in GCC: an evaluation', The Arab Gulf Journal, vol. 6, no. 1, April 1986, pp. 33-42.

33.   Imady, M. 'The role of Arab development funds', The Arab Gulf Journal, vol. 2, no. 2, October 1982, pp. 27-40.

34.   'Inter-Arab co-operation - migration and investment', OAPEC Bulletin, vol. 12, no. 6, June 1986, pp. 6-13.

35.   'Jordan government bond issue', Petro-Money Report, Arab Microfiche Institution, 12 May, 1978.

36.   Kassam, O. 'The Gulf needs creative financial engineering', Euromoney, July 1981, p. 127.

37.   Kassam, O. 'Free the markets and develop', Euromoney, May 1983, pp. 136-47.

38.   Khawaja, A., 'Stock exchange: industrial shares represent 70% of total transactions', Arab Economist, no. 104, May 1978, pp. 8-9.

39.   Khouja, M. 'Arab international co-operation in investment', Dinar, vol. 11, no. 4, 1983, pp. 11-13.

40.   Khouri, R. 'Jordan banking nears maturity', The Middle East, June 1979, pp. 106-8.

41.   Khouri, R. 'Jordan is adapting to the squeeze', Euromoney, May 1985, pp. 256-7.

42.   Kindelberger, C. 'European economic integration

and the development of a single financial centre for long term capital', Weltwirtschaftliches Archive, no. 2, 1963, pp. 189-210.

43.   'Kuwait inaugurates parallel stock market', Middle East Economic Survey, vol. 28, no. 4, 5 November, 1984, p. 31.

44.   'Kuwait investment income drops', Middle East Economic Survey, vol. 28, no. 14, 14 January, 1985, p. 37.

45.   'Kuwait market turnover KD 70 m in first half', Middle East Economic Survey, vol. 27, no. 39, 9 July, 1984, p. 32.

46.   'Kuwaiti securities market needs better organization', Arab Economist, vol. 3, no. 247, December 1981, pp. 30-4.

47.   'Kuwaiti stock market despair', Mid East Markets, vol. 11, no. 14, 20 August, 1984, pp. 6-8.

48.   'Kuwaiti stock market round-up', The Middle East, 30 June, 1980, pp. 5-6.

49.   'Kuwait's stock market in 1979', Mid East Markets, 14 January, 1979, pp. 9-11.

50.   'Kuwait: the new stock exchange', Mid East Markets, vol. 11, no. 22, October 1984, pp. 6-9.

51.   Larre, R. 'Facts of life about the integration of national capital markets', Journal of Money, Credit, Banking, August 1969, pp. 319-27.

52.   'Local stock market stagnates', Mid East Markets, 14 May, 1984, pp. 8-9.

53.   'Lower fees are welcome news to Amman investors', Middle East Economic Digest, vol. 27, no. 3, 1983, p. 28.

54.   Markowski, E. and Markowski, C. 'Concepts, theory and techniques', Decision Sciences Atlanta, vol.16, no. 3, 1985, pp.237-47.

55.   Meek, P. 'International financial integration', Federal Reserve Bank of Atlanta, vol. 70, 1985, pp. 30-5.

56.   Mendelson, M. 'The Eurobond and capital market integration', Journal of Finance, vol. 27, no. 1, 1972, pp. 110-26.

57.   Michael, R. and Edmund, O. 'In search of the Saudi investors', Middle East Economic Digest, vol. 29, no. 2, 11 January, 1985, pp. 12-14.

58.   Mohamed, H. 'Securities and mobilization of savings in Egypt', Investment Review, vol. 3, no. 2, July 1982, p. 8.

59.   Moosa, L. 'An evaluation of Kuwait's monetary

policy and suggestions', Middle East Economic Survey, vol. 28, no. 24, 25 March, 1985, pp. 11-16.

60.   Narpati, B. 'Financial markets in the EEC', Common Market, vol. 7, no. 1, 1967, pp. 13-18.

61.   Nashashibi, H. and Kaseim, O. 'Bringing Kuwait's financial markets up to date', Euromoney, August 1977, pp. 7-11.

62.   Nashashibi, H. 'Financial resources for development; capital markets in developing countries: a study on borrowing by developing countries in the emerging capital markets of the Middle East', OAPEC Bulletin, vol. 6, no. 10, October 1980, pp. 21-34.

63.   Nashashibi, H. 'Major developments in the Arab financial intermediation', OAPEC Bulletin, vol. 6, no. 1, January 1980, pp. 15-24.

64.   Nashashibi, H. 'Investing Arab financial surpluses in the 1980s', OAPEC Bulletin, vol. 6, no. 4, April 1980, pp. 14-16.

65.   Nashashibi, H. 'Arab investing in Japanese equities', OAPEC Bulletin, vol. 7, no. 3, March 1981, pp. 19-22.

66.   Nashashibi, H. 'The changing role of Arab capital markets', Dinar, vol. 1, no. 2, 1981, pp. 28-31.

67.   Nashasibi, H. 'The development and integration of Arab capital markets', OAPEC Bulletin, vol. 8, no. 11, November 1982, pp. 21-8.

68.   Nashashibi, H. 'Challenges confronting Arab banking and Arab capital markets', The Arab Gulf Journal, vol. 4, no. 2, October 1984, pp. 63-71.

69.   Nashashibi, H. 'An Arab capital market: the next step for Arab banking', The Banker, vol. 134, no. 706, December 1984, p. 77.

70.   Nashashibi, H. and Kassem, O. 'An Arab first on Wall Street', The Middle East, December 1985, pp. 24-5.

71.   Nashashibi, H. 'Arab to Arab Eurobonds can work', Euromoney, May 1985, pp. 247-8.

72.   Nashashibi, H. 'Arab involvement in a rapidly changing Euromarket', The Arab Gulf Journal, vol. 5, no. 2, October 1985, pp. 65-71.

73.   'New financial market opens', Middle East Economic Digest, vol. 26, no. 9, 26 February, 1982, p. 33.

74.   'New law aims to stimulate investment', Middle East Economic Digest, vol. 26, no. 40, 1 October, 1982, p. 27.

75.   'New realities: better legal structures and a more

liberal attitude to the secondary markets are needed if Jordan's economy is to readjust to leaner times', Arab Banking and Finance, March 1984, pp. 23-9.

76. 'The new stock exchange', Mid East Markets, 29 October, 1984. pp. 6-9.

77. 'Performance of securities exchange', Aramtek Mid East Monthly, Arab Microfiche Institution, March 1979.

78. Philip, A. 'The integration of financial markets in Western Europe', Journal of Common Market Studies, June 1979, pp. 302-22.

79. Pinder, J. 'Positive integration and negative integration: some problems of economic union in the EEC', The World Today, vol. 24, no. 3, March 1968, p. 90.

80. Poulson, B. and Wallace, M. 'Regional integration in the Middle East: the evidence for trade and capital flows', Middle East Journal, no. 4, 1979, pp. 464-78.

81. 'Real asset: Kuwait's answer to investment', The Middle East, Arab Microfiche Institution, April 1981.

82. 'Regulating the stock market', Euromoney, November 1984, pp. 125-7.

83. 'Regulation of securities and company formation in Kuwait', Middle East Executive Reports, Arab Microfiche Institution, January 1982.

84. Richebacher, K. 'Structural weaknesses of Europe's capital markets', Banker, 117 (502), 1967, pp. 1048-55.

85. Richebacher, K. 'The problems and prospects of integration of European capital markets', Journal of Money, Credit, Banking, August 1969, pp. 336-46.

86. Ripley, D. 'Systematic elements in the linkage of national stock market indices', Review of Economics and Statistics, no. 55, 1973, pp. 356-61.

87. 'The role of investment companies in development in the capital market in Egypt', Investment Review, vol. 4, no. 2, July 1983, pp. 4-5.

88. Rolfe, S. 'The capital market phenomena', Journal of Money, Credit, Banking, August 1969, pp. 332-6.

89. Ross, S. 'Lower fees are welcome news to Amman investors', Middle East Economic Digest, vol. 27, no. 3, 21 January, 1983, p. 28.

90. 'Rules of shareholding', Middle East Executive Report, January 1982, pp. 13-14.

91. Sabbagh, N. 'The revival of the Egyptian stock market', Euromoney, March 1976, pp. 24-6.

92. Santa Maria, A. 'European financial integration',

Giornale degli Economist e Amali di Economica, vol. 40, no. 9, September 1981, pp. 761-73.

93.   'Saudi Arabia by-passes stock market dealings', *An-Nahar Arab Report and Memo*, vol. 8, no. 22, 9 January, 1984, p. 22.

94.   'Saudi Arabia: regulation of the stock market', *Euromoney*, November 1984, pp. 125-7.

95.   'Securities and mobilization of savings in Egypt', *Investment Review*, vol. 3, no. 2, 1982, p. 8.

96.   Segre, C. 'Financial markets in the EEC; prospects for integration', *Moorgate and Wall Street*, August 1983, pp. 38-62.

97.   Schmitt, H. 'Capital markets and the unification of Europe', *World Politics*, January 1986, pp. 228-44.

98.   Scott, I. 'Prospects for the direct integration of EEC capital markets', *Banca Nazionale del Lavoro Quarterly*, June 1967, pp. 178-89.

99.   Scott, I. 'The problems and prospects of integration of European capital markets', *Journal of Money, Credit, Banking*, August 1969, pp. 350-4.

100.   Shireff, D. 'No-one's trading Bahraini shares', *Euromoney*, May 1984, pp. 169-71.

101.   Shireff, D. 'New life for Egypt's stock exchanges', *Euromoney*, May 1984, pp. 183-4.

102.   Shireff, D. 'Sama's stock dilemma', *Euromoney*, May 1984, pp. 158-63.

103.   Shireff, D. 'The flight into Egypt', *Euromoney*, May 1984, pp. 173-81.

104.   'The stock exchange', *Investment Review*, vol. 5, no. 2, July 1984, p. 3.

105.   'Stock exchange activity drops', *Middle East Economic Digest*, vol. 24, no. 34, 22 August, 1980, p. 28.

106.   'Stock exchange dealings top 17.5 m', *The Middle East Reporter*, Arab Microfiche Institution, 10 January, 1979.

107.   'Stock exchange registers five-fold growth', *Middle East Report*, Arab Microfiche Institution, 26 May, 1979.

108.   'Stock exchange revived', *Middle East Economic Digest*, vol. 26, no. 7, 12 February, 1982, p. 12.

109.   'Stock exchange takes shape', *Middle East Economic Digest*, Special Report, September 1983, p. 47.

110.   'Stock market faces risk of collapse due to Iran-Iraq war', *Agefi Review*, Arab Microfiche Institution, 28 September, 1980.

111. 'Stock market growth continued', <u>Middle East Economic Digest</u>, vol. 25, no. 12, 20 March, 1981, pp. 12-16.

112. 'Stock market round-up', <u>Mid East Markets</u>, Arab Microfiche Institution, 30 June, 1980.

113. 'Stock market trading up 182%', <u>Middle East Economic Digest</u>, vol. 24, no. 2, 11 January, 1980, p. 30.

114. Subrahmanyam, M. 'On the optimality of international capital market integration', Journal of Financial Economics, 2, 1975, pp. 40-5.

115. 'Suez canal investment trust', <u>Cotton Outlook</u>, Arab Microfiche Institution, 18 October, 1954.

116. Tarbush, S. 'Arab finance and funds', <u>Dirauna Wal-Alam</u>, Supplement 65, May 1986, pp. 2-6.

117. 'Waiting in the wings', <u>Arab Banking and Finance</u>, July 1983, pp. 26-9.

118. Whelan, J. 'Kuwait stock exchange', <u>Middle East Economic Digest</u>, Practical Guide, 1985, pp. 88-9.

119. 'Will Beirut remain financial centre of the Middle East?', Investors Chronicle, 21 March, 1975. pp. 59-60.

120. Williams, D. 'The development of capital markets in Europe', <u>International Monetary Fund Staff Paper</u>, xii, March 1965, pp. 60-5.

D. NEWSPAPERS

1. 'American expected here to discuss exchange plan', <u>Daily Star</u>, Arab Microfiche Institution, 26 September 1969.

2. 'Amman exchange forecasts 30 per cent growth in 1979', <u>Al-Arab</u>, Arab Microfiche Institution, 15 January 1979.

3. Ayish, M. 'Stock market', <u>Jordan Times</u>, Arab Microfiche Institution, 8 March 1981.

4. 'Banking and finance in the Arab world', <u>Herald International Tribune</u>, A Special Report - Part II, 30 September 1983, pp. 9-16.

5. 'Beirut stock exchange idle for a day', <u>Egyptian Gazette</u>, 5 February 1966, Arab Microfiche Institution.

6. 'Beirut stock exchange idle as brokers go on strike', <u>Daily Star</u>, Arab Microfiche Institution, 16 October 1968.

7. Bonar, J. 'New investment bank will develop capital markets in Jordan', <u>Jordan Times</u>, Arab Microfiche Institution, 7 April 1978.

8. 'Cairo and Alexandria stock markets doubts about future re-opening', Financial Times, Arab Microfiche Institution, 25 July 1961.

9. 'Cairo stock exchange to be re-opened immediately', Egyptian Gazette, Arab Microfiche Institution, 31 March 1977.

10. Downton, E. 'Beirut stock exchange idle in bank crisis', Daily Telegrah, Arab Microfiche Institution, 18 October 1966.

11. Field, P. 'Egypt needs capital market', Financial Times, Arab Microfiche Institution, 10 June 1976.

12. Hagerty, B. 'Bahrain hopes to create a stock exchange', Herald International Tribune, a Special Report, Part II, 30 September 1983, p. 13.

13. Hajjaj, A. 'Beirut may have new stock exchange centre orders will be handled for New York', Daily Star, Arab Microfiche Institution, 27 July 1969.

14. Heller, B. 'Saudi Arabia keeps tight rein on flourishing stock market', Herald International Tribune, a Special Report, Part II, 30 September 1983, pp. 9-10.

15. Hughes, P. 'Financial market looks to the future', Jordan Times, Arab Microfiche Institution, 6 July 1981.

16. Jaber, T. 'Turning financial to real investment', Jordan Times, Arab Microfiche Institution, 25 January 1982.

17. Karam, F. 'Beirut's finance centre?' Daily Star, Arab Microfiche Institution, 1 December 1974.

18. Khouri, R. 'Activity on stock exchange expected to double this year', Jordan Times, Arab Microfiche Institution, 8 May 1979.

19. Khouri, R. 'Volume of Amman stock exchange trading will top 17.5 m in first year', Financial Times, Arab Microfiche Institution, 18 December 1978.

20. 'Kuwait stock market report', Arab Times, Arab Microfiche Institution, 23 January 1980.

21. 'Ministry IFC study stock exchange', Egyptian Mail, Arab Microfiche Institution, 6 December 1975.

22. 'Move to develop stock exchange', Egyptian Gazette, Arab Microfiche Institution, 3 May 1977.

23. 'Need to regulate Kuwait stock market', Arab Times, Arab Microfiche Institution, 13 February 1982.

24. 'New Amman stock exchange makes five-fold increase', Arab News, Arab Microfiche Institution, 26 May 1978.

25. 'New listing rules for Kuwait's stock market', Gulf Daily News, Arab Microfiche Institution, 1 November 1980.

26. 'Planning Ministry prepares study on volume, movement of capital in Lebanon's markets', Daily Telegraph, Arab Microfiche Institution, 4 September 1970.

27. 'Report said received by Premier Yaffi on stock exchange market conditions here', Arab World, Arab Microfiche Institution, 31 May 1966.

28. Said, J. 'Fakhourg discusses Lebanese stock market investors', Daily Star, Arab Microfiche Institution, 1981.

29. 'Stock exchange off to fast start', Financial Times, Arab Microfiche Institution, 26 May 1978.

30. Tohamy, O. 'Cairo capital market: stimulation is needed', Herald International Tribune, a Special Report, Part II, 30 September 1983, p. 11.

31. 'As trading on stock exchange hits 2.5 m a month, officials eye freer investments from Gulf', Financial Times, Arab Microfiche Institution, 25 September 1978.

32. 'Trading slow at stock exchange', Jordan Times, Arab Microfiche Institution, 3 January 1979.

E. CONFERENCES

1. Cohen, M. A large capital market: the American experience, paper presented at a Conference on 'The integration of European securities markets', organised by L'Universite Internationale des Sciences, Luxembourg, 19-20 November 1971.

2. Nashashibi, H. Financial resources for development capital markets in developing countries: a study on borrowing by developing countries in the emerging capital markets of the Middle East, paper presented at a Conference on 'Trade and Development' organised by the United Nations, Geneva, 3 July 1980.

3. Nashashibi, H. Medium and long-term finance in the Arab capital markets, (in Arabic), paper presented at a Conference on 'Capital markets in the Arab states, their reality and their prospect of development', organised by the Arab Monetary Fund, Abu Dhabi, 4-6 February 1984.

4. Wareham, W. The supervision and regulation of security markets in the EEC, paper presented at a Conference on 'The integration of European securities markets', organised by the London Stock Exchange, Brussels, 11 October 1972.

F   REPORTS

1.   Commission of the EEC, <u>The development of a European capital market</u>, Report by a group of experts under the direction of C. Segre, Brussels, November 1966.

2.   Commission of the EEC, <u>Control of securities markets in the European economic community</u>, Report on a Comparative Law Study submitted by Wymeersch, R., Brussels, December 1977.

3.   Werner, <u>Rapport au conseil et a la Commission sur la réalisation par étapes de l'union economique et monétaire de la communauté</u>, 8 October 1970. Supplement au bulletin des Communautés Européennes, 11, 1970.

INDEX